Books Written or Edited by
LEONARD S. MARCUS

Petrouchka, illustrated by Jane Kendall (1983)

Picture Books (1984)

An Épinal Album: Popular Prints from Nineteenth-Century France (editor, 1984)

Humor and Play in Children's Literature (editor, 1989)

Mother Goose's Little Misfortunes, illustrated by Amy Schwartz (editor, 1990)

Margaret Wise Brown: Awakened by the Moon (1992)

Lifelines: A Poetry Anthology (editor, 1994)

75 Years of Children's Book Week Posters (1994)

Morrow Junior Books: The First Fifty Years (1996)

The Making of Goodnight Moon: A Fiftieth Anniversary Retrospective (1997)

A Caldecott Celebration: Six Artists and Their Paths to the Caldecott Medal (1998)

Dear Genius: The Letters of Ursula Nordstrom (editor, 1998)

Author Talk (2000)

Side by Side: Five Favorite Picture Book Teams Go to Work (2001)

Ways of Telling: Conversations on the Art of the Picture Book (2002)

Storied City: A Children's Book Walking-Tour Guide to New York City (2003)

The Wand in the Word: Conversations with Writers of Fantasy (2006)

Oscar: The Big Adventure of a Little Sock Monkey, co-authored with Amy Schwartz; illustrated by Amy Schwartz (2006)

Pass It Down: Five Picture-Book Families Make Their Mark (2007)

A Caldecott Celebration: Seven Artists and Their Paths to the Caldecott Medal (2008)

Minders of Make-Believe: Idealists, Entrepreneurs, and the Shaping of American Children's Literature (2008)

Funny Business: Conversations with Writers of Comedy (2009)

The Annotated Phantom Tollbooth (editor, 2011)

Show Me a Story! Why Picture Books Matter (2012)

Listening for Madeleine: A Portrait of Madeleine L'Engle in Many Voices (2012)

Maurice Sendak: A Celebration of the Artist and His Work (editor, 2013)

Comics Confidential: Thirteen Graphic Novelists Talk Story, Craft, and Life Outside the Box (2016)

The Runaway Bunny: A 75th Anniversary Retrospective (2017)

Golden Legacy: The Story of Golden Books (2007/2017)

The Kairos Novels, by Madeleine L'Engle (editor, 2018)

Helen Oxenbury: A Life in Illustration (2019)

100 Years of Children's Book Week Posters (2019)

The ABC of It: Why Children's Books Matter (2019)

You Can't Say That!: Writers for Young People Talk about Censorship, Free Expression, and the Stories They Have to Tell (2021)

Mr. Lincoln Sits for His Portrait: The Story of a Photograph that Became an American Icon (2023)

MR. LINCOLN
SITS FOR HIS
PORTRAIT

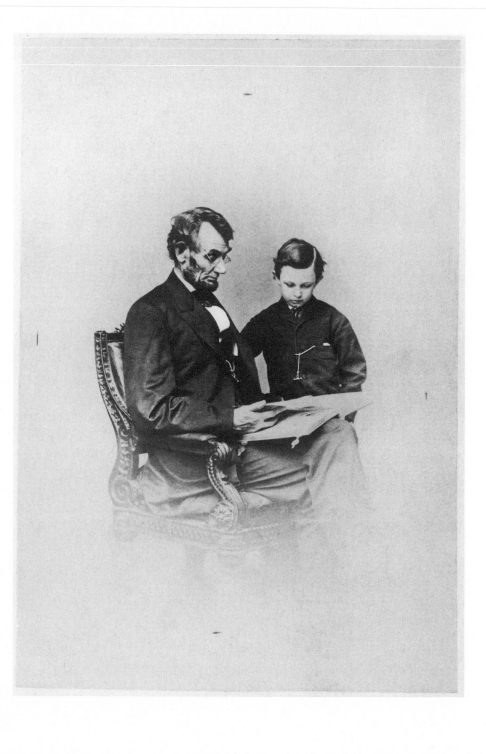

Leonard S. Marcus

MR. LINCOLN SITS FOR HIS PORTRAIT

The Story of a Photograph
That Became an American Icon

FARRAR STRAUS GIROUX
NEW YORK

Farrar Straus Giroux Books for Young Readers
An imprint of Macmillan Publishing Group, LLC
120 Broadway, New York, NY 10271 • mackids.com
Copyright © 2023 by Leonard S. Marcus. All rights reserved.

Our books may be purchased in bulk for promotional, educational, or business use.
Please contact your local bookseller or the Macmillan Corporate and Premium Sales
Department at (800) 221-7945 ext. 5442 or by email at
MacmillanSpecialMarkets@macmillan.com.

Library of Congress Cataloging-in-Publication Data
Names: Marcus, Leonard S., 1950– author.
Title: Mr. Lincoln sits for his portrait : the story of a photograph that
became an American icon / Leonard S. Marcus.
Other titles: Story of a photograph that became an American icon
Description: First edition. | New York : Farrar Straus Giroux, 2023. | Includes
bibliographical references and index. | Audience: Ages 10–12 | Audience: Grades
4–6 | Summary: "A middle-grade nonfiction book about one of America's most
historically resonant images, the circumstances surrounding its creation, and the
larger story it tells about Abraham Lincoln's life"— Provided by publisher.
Identifiers: LCCN 2022013851 | ISBN 9780374303488 (hardcover)
Subjects: LCSH: Lincoln, Abraham, 1809–1865—Portraits—Juvenile literature. |
Presidents—United States—Portraits—Juvenile literature. | Portrait photography—
United States—History—19th century—Juvenile literature. | United States—
Politics and government—1861–1865—Juvenile literature.
Classification: LCC E457.6 .M23 2023 | DDC 973.7—dc23/eng/20220525
LC record available at https://lccn.loc.gov/2022013851

First edition, 2023

Book design by Mallory Grigg and Maria Williams
Printed in the United States of America by Lakeside Book Company,
Crawfordsville, Indiana

1 3 5 7 9 10 8 6 4 2

Frontispiece: Photograph of President Lincoln and his son Tad by Anthony Berger, February 9, 1864

Remembering David Brion Davis

Historian, teacher, guide

CONTENTS

MR. LINCOLN
SITS FOR HIS
PORTRAIT

M. B. BRADY'S

Photographic Gallery of Art,

NEW YORK CITY,

AND

352 PENNSYLVANIA AVENUE,

WASHINGTON, D. C.

Every style of

PORTRAIT,

FROM THE SMALLEST LOCKET SIZE

TO THE FULL SIZE OF LIFE,

EXECUTED IN THE VERY BEST STYLE OF THE ART.

We have Artists—who excel in their line—devoted specially to each branch of the various departments of coloring in Oil, India Ink, Water Color and the other fine Tints given to Pictures done at this establishment.

Artists always ready to go at a moment's notice and take views of Camps, Groupes, Deceased Persons, Dwellings, Public Buildings, &c.

PHOTOGRAPHS,
AMBROTYPES,
SOUVENIRS,
DAGUERREOTYPES,
CARTES DE VISITE,

And all the different styles of pictures, either plain or highly colored.

PICTURES COPIED SUCCESSFULLY.

A. BERGER, Manager.

Advertisement for the studios of America's most illustrious Civil War–era portrait photographer, Mathew Brady, from an 1864 Washington, DC, business directory, with Anthony Berger listed as manager.

INTRODUCTION

For one who thought so little of his own looks and was so often mocked for his appearance by others, Abraham Lincoln loved the camera. Lincoln sat for his first portrait in 1846 or 1847, a few short years after the invention of photographic portraiture, and repeated the experience over one hundred more times between then and 1865, the year he died.

Lincoln was not, by anyone's account, a foolish or vain man but rather a shrewd and deeply purposeful one. He had had next to no formal schooling but was born with a hungry mind, read voraciously, and understood sooner than most the shape-changing import of the mechanical marvels with which the inventors of his day were expanding people's horizons: the railroad, by dramatically shrinking travel times, redefining *fast* and *far*, and knitting the nation together in a strong and ultimately unbreakable web; the telegraph, by making the news of any given locale knowable everywhere in a matter of seconds or at most of minutes or hours; photography, by harnessing light and arresting time itself to capture strangely lifelike images of people and places.

Lincoln made brilliant use of all these new technologies in his climb from backwoods politician to the summit of the US presidency. Once there, he used them again to direct a far-flung war and begin the healing process for a divided Union. Although

In this detail of what is thought to be the first photo he ever posed for, from 1846 or 1847, Lincoln looks frozen stiff and perhaps ready to stretch his long legs.

a spellbinding speaker, he let the photographs he posed for do much of his talking by showing himself to the world as a man of strength, conviction, humility, and compassion—and not the devil his enemies claimed.

But did photographs never lie? As Lincoln himself learned by patient trial and error, every photograph has a point of view, revealing some facets of its subject and missing or glossing over others. The strongest photographs possess the power to crowd out competing perspectives and become the version of reality that people remember.

As it happens, six of the photographic portraits of Abraham Lincoln that the world remembers best were made by the same photographer, Anthony Berger, on the same day, February 9, 1864.

This is the story of that day and one of those pictures.

1

RIDER IN THE WOODS

Abraham Lincoln had his audience right where he wanted them: in the palm of his hand. A lone rider, he had told the roomful of newspaper editors, was picking his way along a narrow path in the Illinois woods. Poor fellow, Lincoln chuckled. He was "not possessed of features the ladies would call handsome."

Just then, a woman approached on horseback from the opposite direction and the man reined back his horse to let her pass. He supposed a simple thank-you might be in order, but instead the woman spoke up sharply in complaint. "Well, for land sake," she growled, "you are the homeliest man I ever saw."

"Yes, madam," replied the sorry fellow, "but I cannot help it."

"No, I suppose not," said the woman before riding on, "but you might stay at home."

The year was 1856, and Lincoln, a well-regarded trial lawyer and former congressman, was speaking to a convention of Illinois newspaper editors, a powerful group whose support he would need should he run for office again one day. The editors roared with laughter at the oddball tale but were left wondering afterward: Had Lincoln himself been the man in the story? He might as well have been. Friends and foes alike never tired of making schoolyard fun of his strangely elongated, bony face and gangly, six foot four frame.

"Mr. Lincoln [is] the homeliest man I ever saw," declared a lawyer and journalist who counted himself among Lincoln's admirers. "His body," Donn Piatt could not help adding, "[is like] . . . a huge skeleton in clothes."

Poet Walt Whitman rarely lacked for words, and worshipped Lincoln, but found himself sputtering when confronted with the daunting task of writing an honest description of the man: "He has a face . . . ," Whitman ventured, "so awful ugly it becomes beautiful, with its strange mouth, its deep cut, crisscross lines, and its doughnut complexion."

Lincoln's enemies had far worse things to say, professing their outright disgust at the sight of him, calling Lincoln "altogether repulsive," and likening the general impression he made to that of a "great baboon," as much as to say that Lincoln might not even be fully human.

A Lincoln Timeline, 1809–1858

1809 *Born February 12 at Sinking Spring Farm, LaRue County, Kentucky, the second child of Thomas Lincoln* *and Nancy Hanks Lincoln. Sister Sarah is two years older.*

1811–1816 *The Lincolns move twice, resettling in rural Indiana.*

1818 *Mother dies of "milk sickness," a kind of food poisoning.*

1819 *Father marries Sarah Bush Johnston, a widow with three children.*

1824 *Now in his teens, takes odd jobs to help support the family, attends school when possible, becomes an avid reader.*

1827–1828 *Works on and off as a ferryman and, during a trip down the Mississippi, is deeply disturbed on witnessing a New Orleans slave auction.*

1830 *The Lincolns move to Illinois. Makes first political speech on the topic of improvements needed for efficient river navigation.*

1831 *Works as a shop clerk. Falls in love with Ann Rutledge, who dies of typhus four years later.*

1832 *Runs for Illinois State assemblyman but loses the election. Joins the Illinois Militia, is voted regiment captain, but sees no action in the Black Hawk War.*

1834 *At age 24, becomes a member of the Illinois General Assembly, an office held through 1842. Takes up the study of law.*

1837 *Admitted to the Illinois Bar and begins twice-yearly rounds of state circuit courts. Moves to Springfield,* *the new Illinois state capital, and co-founds a law firm as his career as a trial lawyer flourishes.*

1842 *After an on-again, off-again courtship, marries Mary Todd, daughter of a powerful Kentucky political family.*

1843 *Robert Todd Lincoln, named for Mary's father, is born.*

1844 *The Lincolns purchase a wooden cottage in Springfield.*

1846 *The Lincolns' second son, Eddie, is born. Elected to the US House of Representatives. First known photograph, taken in Springfield, probably late that year.*

1847–1848 *As a congressman, speaks out against the Mexican-American War and slavery. Fails to win reelection.*

1849 *Granted US government patent No. 6,469 for an inflatable device designed to free grounded riverboats from a sandbar.*

1850 *Eddie Lincoln dies. Willie Lincoln is born.*

1851 *Skips the funeral of his often cruel and difficult father, Thomas Lincoln.*

1853 *Thomas (Tad) Lincoln is born.*

1854–1857 *Reenters politics, opposing the pro-slavery Kansas-Nebraska Act of 1854. In 1856, is considered for the vice presidential slot on the ticket of the newly formed Republican Party, but comes in second behind William L. Dayton.*

1858 *Runs for the US Senate, losing to the incumbent Stephen A. Douglas, but attracts widespread national attention for his two-fisted performance during the Lincoln-Douglas Debates that summer and fall.*

In 1844, the Lincolns moved into a modest Springfield cottage and gradually expanded it until it became the stately home seen here. In this photo taken in the summer of 1860, presidential candidate Lincoln can be glimpsed out front with sons Tad (left) and Willie.

Pro-slavery politicians in particular hated Lincoln to the core and wished to destroy his reputation before "Honest Abe," the mighty "Railsplitter"—as his boosters had affectionately tagged him—ever got the chance to win the presidency and make his anti-slavery views the law of the land. At a time when many

Americans believed that every face was a window into its owner's soul, to call Lincoln ugly was to brand him a man of low moral worth and thus a poor choice for high public office.

Lincoln, however, had a few tricks up his own sleeve. Gleefully joining the chorus of his detractors, he blunted the edge of their verbal jibes by gamely suggesting that he agreed with their poor opinion of his helter-skelter looks. Words to that effect became one of his most dependable laugh lines when in 1858 he ran as the Republican candidate for the US Senate from Illinois. All that summer and fall, he took part in a series of marathon debates with his opponent, the smooth-talking incumbent Stephen A. Douglas, and traded barbs in front of thousands of spectators as he laid out his views on the future of America.

Senator Douglas was a stout man, and as short one might say as Lincoln was tall, but he looked every inch the distinguished statesman and legislator. Douglas was also a masterly debater, and at one point he tried to set Lincoln back on his heels by accusing him of having no core beliefs for voters to judge him by, and of cynically telling Illinoisans instead whatever it was he thought they wanted to hear.

Douglas, however, had for once spoken carelessly, and no sooner had he called him "two-faced" than Lincoln, motioning deadpan to himself, declared to squeals of approval from the crowd, "I leave it to my audience: if I had another face, would I be wearing this one?"

Lincoln was the underdog in the race against Douglas and come November he did indeed go down smartly in defeat. But on top of the crowds that had gathered in town squares in every part of the state to witness the gladiatorial battles, newspapers across the nation had published the debate transcripts word for word, and a great many readers who had never heard of Abraham Lincoln before came away mightily impressed.

Lincoln spoke in the folksy, backwoods Kentucky drawl of his youth and in an oddly high-pitched voice that some listeners thought ludicrous coming from such a towering figure. But in print, the plainspoken eloquence of his words was all readers registered; that and the fervor of his convictions (yes, he *did* have convictions about the abolition of slavery, states' rights, and other urgent questions of the day). All that, and the steel-trap force of his intellect and the charm and wisdom of his funny yarns.

In one encounter, after Douglas had rambled on about the many fine and noble people in his family ancestry, Lincoln remarked dryly that he knew next to nothing about his own family, except that he came from a "long line of married folk"—as if to say the low-born Lincolns, much like most ordinary Americans, were lucky to have met even that mundane requirement.

Humor alone, however, could not disarm his enemies or earn him the confidence of voters. As Lincoln emerged from the 1858 election as an up-and-coming national figure, the verbal attacks leveled at him only intensified. (They would persist in some quarters even after the tragic end of his presidency.) One more such comment is worth recalling for the remarkable truth about Lincoln its author had observed.

Honest old Abe on the Stump
Springfield. 1858

Honest old Abe on the Stump
at the ratification Meeting of
Presidential Nomination
Springfield 1860

In this anti-Lincoln political cartoon from the 1860 election season, "Honest Old Abe" does indeed have "two faces," neither of them all that attractive. The character on the left is meant to represent Lincoln in his earlier, humbler days; the one on the right, the supposedly arrogant and cocksure would-be president.

On a visit to Washington in 1862, Colonel Charles Wainwright, a wealthy New York Democrat who was no great admirer of Lincoln, had caught a glimpse of the president at the opera. Writing in his diary later that evening, Wainwright delighted in marking down the occasion as confirmation of his dim view of the commander in chief: "It would be hard work to find the great man in his face or figure," chortled the colonel, echoing the popular notion that a person's character is an open book for all to read, "and he is infinitely uglier than any of his pictures."

Infinitely uglier than any of his pictures . . . Only a few years earlier, Lincoln himself had come to the same conclusion—but had divined an advantage, not a deficit, in the gap between image and reality. By the mid-1850s, it had become clear to him that the written word, and the art of oratory that political leaders had practiced since the days of ancient Greece and Rome, were not the only instruments of persuasion available to him as an ambitious politician on a quest to make himself useful to the nation. Pictures—and most especially photographs, the new wonder of the Industrial Age—had the power to lodge strong and lasting impressions in people's memories and to change their minds.

Photography Invented

Many clever people had a hand in the invention of photography. In the 1820s, a Frenchman named Nicéphore Niépce built a camera that worked well enough but required hours-long exposure times to create a picture. Because nobody can sit still for hours on end, that ruled out taking photos of people—or of anything that moved. By 1839, however, inventors in France and England—Louis Daguerre and William Henry Fox Talbot—had each come up with a much quicker process, and portrait photography was born. People were excited! Everyone wanted to sit for the camera. There was still one problem, though: The Daguerre and Fox Talbot methods each produced only a single print, making it hard or impossible to share

photos with friends. Then in 1851, another Englishman,
Frederick Scott Archer, had an idea that revolutionized
photography. Archer's camera captured an image on a
glass-plate negative from which any number of copies of
the photo could be made. Soon after that, cartes de visite
and other souvenir photos were everywhere—much to the
benefit of a media-savvy politician like Abraham Lincoln.

Not every photograph showed off its subject to the same
good advantage, of course, but the right photo *could*. In arriving
at this understanding, Lincoln was ahead of nearly everybody.
He was the first American politician—and one of the world's
first public figures—to turn to photography as a tool for presenting himself to millions of people he might never have the chance
to meet and uniting them around a common purpose.

2

A FACE TO THE WORLD

Inventions of all kinds fascinated Lincoln.

As a circuit lawyer traveling from town to town in rural Illinois, he took time out to inspect the local farm equipment and fiddle with the machines' complex mechanisms, a hobby of sorts he had acquired from his father. The telegraph—the nineteenth century's astonishing new instant messaging system—so amazed him that he took pleasure in referring to it by its colorful popular nickname: the Lightning.

As president, he tested the army's latest repeating rifles by engaging in target practice with friends on the White House lawn.

He had even briefly been an inventor himself. As a young ferryman on the Ohio and Mississippi rivers, Lincoln had twice run his flatboat aground on a sandbar. Two decades later, as a congressman from Illinois, he recalled the trouble he had had navigating two of America's vital commercial waterways and spent his recess break designing a floatable device for use in freeing stranded vessels.

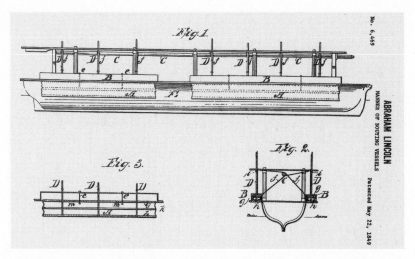

No. 6,469

ABRAHAM LINCOLN

MANNER OF BUOYING VESSELS

Patented May 22, 1849

Lincoln's bright idea was to fit the bottom of a boat with a series of inflatable bags (A) that, when filled with air, expanded from beneath wooden storage boxes (B) and would raise a stranded vessel high enough to free it from a sandbar. Lincoln helped build a wooden model himself and was proud of his invention, even though it was never manufactured. He remains the only president to have held a US government patent.

When the government granted Lincoln a patent for his invention in 1849, the good news arrived as a kind of consolation prize after his failed reelection bid and return to the practice of law, his political career having seemingly run aground after one meager term.

It had been in happier days, not long after his election to the House of Representatives, that Lincoln visited a Springfield photographer's studio to sit for his first known portrait. Winning a House seat was an occasion worth commemorating, and his wife, Mary, who came from a high-born and politically connected Kentucky family, would have understood this even if Lincoln himself did not. She accompanied her husband to the sitting and posed for her own portrait as well, to display beside his in matching frames in their parlor (see color insert).

Lincoln, who did not care much for fashion or finery, had arrived at the session in a stiff black suit with curiously wide lapels that called undue attention to his exaggerated facial features. When it was his turn, he took his place in the sitter's chair next to a table where a leather-bound book had been placed as a symbol of learning.

The chosen camera angle unwittingly made Lincoln's big hands appear almost as large as his long, dour-looking, clean-shaven face. Lincoln must not have been too pleased with the result; the next known portrait of him came eight years later and was taken in Chicago.

In the 1840s, photography was still in its infancy and innovators on both sides of the Atlantic were scrambling to patent the latest techniques and equipment for drawing light to a chemically treated surface and capturing an image from the real world. In the case of one popular early type of photography, called the daguerreotype method, the camera yielded only a single, one-of-a-kind print on a shimmering sheet of silvered copper.

A revolutionary advance came with the introduction of methods that produced an intermediary "negative" from which an unlimited number of copies of the same image could be made. Negatives greatly expanded the opportunities for photographers to turn their work into a viable business, as became abundantly clear when a wild craze swept Europe and the United States for inexpensive, playing card–size photographic portraits known by their French term as cartes de visite or calling cards.

Only the rich could afford to have their portraits painted in oil in the traditional way. But just about everyone could have their own carte de visite made—and keep an ample supply of the cards on hand for giving out to friends, family, and business associates. People collected one another's cards and proudly displayed their collections in elaborate leather-bound albums left out on parlor tables for guests to admire.

The popular fashion expanded to encompass an early form of celebrity fandom, as photo studios made a sideline of selling carte-style images of all the famous people of the day: everyone

In his second-known portrait, taken in late 1854, Lincoln again sits stiffly in place, this time with his bow tie clownishly off-kilter. But his tousled hair is a delightfully human touch that suggests he is starting to warm to the idea of being himself for the camera.

from novelists, poets, inventors, actors, and military heroes to senators, Supreme Court justices, and presidents.

Lincoln himself seems not to have become a collector, but after a second, more positive experience before the camera in Chicago in 1854, he steadily warmed to the role of photographic subject. He sat for fourteen or more portraits over the next half-dozen years, the period when, besides solidifying his reputation as a trial lawyer, he reentered politics as a member of the Illinois state legislature and candidate for the United States Senate.

It must have amused him to see how many versions of himself the camera eye was capable of observing. In some photos, Lincoln looks tired or distracted, or is caught with his black silk bow tie in disarray or his big floppy ears poking out unattractively.

But one rather grand yet disarmingly casual portrait taken in 1857 pleased him enormously, prompting Lincoln to declare it a "very true" likeness. "Though," he ruefully noted, "my wife, and many others, do not [agree]. My impression is that their objection arises from the disordered condition of the hair."

Mid-nineteenth-century American newspapers did not yet have the technical know-how to publish photographs directly in their pages, so they employed artists to make detailed line engravings based on newsworthy photos and published those instead. Adapted in this way, the photographs of important people and events often reached a vast audience. Cartes de visite images copied from a photographic portrait might multiply that photograph's impact many more times over.

The great turning point in Lincoln's embrace of photography came in February of 1860, during a whirlwind trip to New York City. Lincoln arrived in the thrumming commercial metropolis still something of a mystery man in the minds of many. Supporters were touting him as a potential candidate in the upcoming presidential election that year. But Lincoln had not yet declared his intention to run, and those who hoped he would not run loudly proclaimed that he lacked the political skills and polish to lead the nation.

The main purpose of Lincoln's trip was to deliver a speech on the evening of February 27 in the Great Hall of the Cooper Union, one of the city's largest and most prestigious public venues. Nearly fifteen hundred people crowded into the auditorium to hear, or perhaps just gawk at, the lanky Westerner as he elaborated his thoughts on the future of slavery—a topic that had grown ever more urgent as the country drifted toward civil war.

In this 1857 photo taken in Chicago, Lincoln has finally got the hang of it, presenting himself as a strong, down-to-earth, and self-confident man — relaxed but ready for action. Lincoln liked this portrait a lot, but Mary Lincoln thought he should have combed his hair.

The Cooper Union opened in 1859 as an exciting experiment in democratic education: a tuition-free college where talented young men and women of modest means could train for careers in architecture, engineering, and the arts. An idealist and inventor, founder Peter Cooper envisioned the school's Great Hall as a grand showcase for America's most creative thinkers in politics and culture. For Lincoln, it was the perfect stage from which to launch a bid for the presidency.

Lincoln had taken more time than usual writing his address, knowing he would be speaking not just to the New Yorkers who came that evening but to the entire nation. As he strode awkwardly onstage and up to the lectern ornately draped in velvet, Lincoln, a devoted theatergoer, understood he was there to give the audition of his life.

Hours earlier, Lincoln's Republican Club hosts had arranged a photo session for him at the nearby Mathew Brady studio on lower Broadway. A striking portrait would prove invaluable if Lincoln did decide to run, and no photographer in America could be counted on to do the job better.

Some visitors came to Mathew Brady's posh New York gallery just to browse, but many stayed to have their pictures taken and to shop for collectible photos of their heroes and favorite celebrities.

Brady's fame, in fact, far exceeded Lincoln's own at the time; leading the honor roll of his illustrious subjects was every president of the United States since John Quincy Adams, the sole exception being William Henry Harrison, who had died of pneumonia after serving only one month in office, and before a sitting could be arranged.

Brady could size up a subject at a glance, and as the rangy Western politician stepped through the doorway of his elegant studio, he saw that he had his work cut out for him. Mary Lincoln

Mathew Brady

The son of Irish immigrants, Mathew Brady (ca. 1823– 1896) grew up in upstate New York and fell in love with painting as a teenager. He followed his dream to New York City just as photography was becoming the new art sensation and learned all about cameras from the inventor of the telegraph, Samuel F. B. Morse.

Opting to make portrait photography his professional specialty, Brady opened a studio and soon had everyone from Daniel Webster to Edgar Allan Poe and Abraham Lincoln lining up to have their picture taken by him. Never a modest man, Brady crowed that his photographs would one day be hailed as a national treasure.

He was right. Today Brady's portraits are prized as an incomparable pictorial record of the notable Americans of his age, and his Civil War battlefield photographs are admired and studied as landmark works in the history of photojournalism.

The dapper photographer in a portrait taken by a member of his staff, ca. 1861.

later spoke of the gloomy "photographer's face" that washed over her husband's features whenever he sat for the camera.

Further complicating matters was Lincoln's chronic indifference to his own appearance even when, as on this occasion, he came dressed in a well-fitting black suit that he probably bought for the occasion. Brady opted to pull the camera back for a long view and had Lincoln stand in front of a classical column, with one hand firmly perched on a book. When the pose was just about set, it suddenly occurred to Brady to ask Lincoln to pull up his shirt collar.

"Ah," came the knowing reply, "you want to shorten my neck."

"That's just it," said the photographer a bit sheepishly, but also sounding greatly relieved, after which the two men had a good laugh.

What happened next was photographic magic. The Brady portrait caught a look of unwavering determination in Lincoln's gaze and physical presence. Here, it announced, was a true leader. Here was someone the nation could trust.

That evening, as Lincoln concluded his speech with a rousing declaration—"Let us have faith that right makes might, and in that faith let us, to the end, dare to do our duty as we understand it"—his audience stomped and cheered their assent and came away with much the same idea of him.

As word of his powerful Cooper Union address spread across America, demand for pictures of Lincoln soared. With civil war a real possibility, the message of Mathew Brady's February 1860 portrait was clear and well timed to the moment: "I am ready to lead."

HARPER'S WEEKLY.

A JOURNAL OF CIVILIZATION.

Vol. IV.—No. 178.]   NEW YORK, SATURDAY, MAY 26, 1860.   [Price Five Cents.

Entered according to Act of Congress, in the Year 1860, by Harper & Brothers, in the Clerk's Office of the District Court for the Southern District of New York.

HON. ABRAM LINCOLN, OF ILLINOIS.

[REPUBLICAN CANDIDATE FOR PRESIDENT.]

We engrave herewith the portrait—from a photograph by Brady—of Hon. Abram Lincoln, of Illinois, the Republican candidate for President. The following sketch of his career is from the *Herald*:

HON. ABRAM LINCOLN, OF ILLINOIS, REPUBLICAN CANDIDATE FOR PRESIDENT.

[Photographed by Brady.]

Following Lincoln's nomination for president, Brady allowed *Harper's Weekly*, a widely read news magazine, to adapt the photo for its cover illustration. Lincoln could not have asked for better publicity.

3

THE FUTURE IN FOCUS

It has often been said that Lincoln's dazzlingly well-reasoned Cooper Union address and Brady's portrait of the same day were the two main factors that won him the White House.

Events unfolded rapidly after that. In mid-May, Lincoln became the Republican Party's presidential nominee. By then, the Brady photo had gone viral as a highly prized carte de visite. Immediately after the nominating convention, the photo morphed again, appearing as a line engraving on the cover of *Harper's Weekly*. Lincoln was accustomed to having his words flashed by the Lightning to newspapers across America. Now his picture was everywhere, too, including on the front page of the widely read magazine that billed itself as the "journal of civilization."

Presidential campaigns of the mid-nineteenth century bore almost no resemblance to the media spectacles they later became. The candidate was expected to stay at home and meet with visiting delegations of supporters from around the country, who would go back and work on his behalf, presumably in return for promised favors.

The Speech That Changed Lincoln's Life

Lincoln knew he had a lot riding on his Cooper Union address and made sure to do his homework. His subject was the question then on every American's mind: the future of slavery. America's vast Western territories were being carved up into new states (Kansas would become a state in 1861, Nevada in 1864), and West Virginia was formed from former Virginia territory in 1863. People asked: Should slavery be allowed in the new states or not? Lincoln's party, the Republicans, said no, while their main opponents, the Democrats, said the voters in each new state should decide for themselves. To bolster their case, Democrats insisted that the Founding Fathers would surely have agreed with them. But at the Cooper Union, Lincoln went down the list of the signers of the US Constitution and, citing their actions and words, showed this claim to be false. It was as though Lincoln had taken an ax to his opponents' defense of slavery and ripped it to shreds. The audience was deeply impressed by the force of his argument and command of the facts, and that evening Lincoln won many new supporters.

Conforming to the custom, Lincoln declined even to give a speech in Bloomington, Illinois, a city less than one hundred miles from Springfield. As he greeted group after group of his supporters at home and wrote letter after letter clarifying his positions, however, he pursued one nontraditional strategy for reaching out to voters as well: Lincoln frequented Springfield's photographers' studios and sat for at least eighteen more portraits.

Throughout the bitter four-way presidential campaign, in which the northern and southern Democrats each fielded candidates and a fourth party also entered the fray, hundreds of surrogates spoke out on Lincoln's behalf. So too, in effect, did the growing abundance of new Lincoln pictures.

An exchange of letters between the candidate and a young fan gives some indication of just how widely images of him were circulating across the country. In mid-October, while still holed up in a borrowed office in the Illinois Statehouse, Lincoln received a letter from eleven-year-old Grace Bedell of Westfield, New York, on the shore of Lake Erie, who urged him to grow a beard to improve his voter appeal. The girl, a daughter of staunch Republicans, had seen a crudely illustrated campaign poster and concluded that Lincoln needed her help:

"If you let your whiskers grow," she said, ". . . you would look a great deal better for your face is so thin. All the ladies like whiskers and would tease their husbands to vote for you and then you would be President."

Four days later, Lincoln wrote a charming response in which he took Grace and her idea seriously enough to share his misgivings about it. After inquiring about her family, he wrote: "As

Wishing to help his election chances, eleven-year-old Grace Bedell wrote to candidate Lincoln on October 18, 1860, urging him to hide his long, bony face behind a beard. Lincoln was charmed by the letter but still on the fence about Grace's plan when he wrote back to her a few days later. By late November, however, Lincoln was game to give it a try.

to the whiskers, having never worn any, do you not think people would call it a silly affectation if I were to begin it now?"

And yet . . . during a trip to Chicago as president-elect in late November, Lincoln performed a secret experiment on himself, arriving with newly grown chin whiskers at a photographer's studio to see what the result might be. His conclusion: Grace

The president-elect photographed in Chicago in late 1860 with the beginnings of a beard.

was right. Several weeks later, he once again sat for a photographer, now with a full beard framing his face—and again on February 9, just two days before he left for his new life in the nation's capital. By Inauguration Day, March 4, 1861, millions of Americans had seen pictures of the newly bearded, and perhaps more presidential-looking, Abraham Lincoln.

A Lincoln Timeline, 1859–1861

1859 *Makes several speeches in and around Illinois in which he opposes the expansion of slavery but does not call for its immediate abolition.*

February 27, 1860 *Photographed by Mathew Brady and gives career-altering speech at New York's Cooper Union on the future of slavery.*

May 18, 1860 *Named Republican candidate for president.*

November 6, 1860 *Elected sixteenth president of the United States.*

February 11, 1861 *Boards a private train in Springfield for a ceremonial, thirteen-day journey to Washington.*

March 4, 1861 *Inaugural address invokes fellow countrymen's "better angels of our nature" in a final appeal to the Southern states to avert civil war.*

April 12, 1861 *Confederate forces fire on Fort Sumter, South Carolina, marking the start of armed conflict.*

July 21, 1861 *Union Army unexpectedly trounced in First Battle of Bull Run, Virginia, suggesting the war might last much longer than previously imagined.*

In the November 10, 1860, issue celebrating Lincoln's electoral victory, *Harper's Weekly* again made use of an engraving of Brady's portrait, this time featuring the entire image and, for variety's sake, having Lincoln face the other way.

By the time Abraham Lincoln arrived in Washington on February 23, 1861, seven Southern states had seceded from the Union, civil war was imminent, and threats against his life had become a commonplace occurrence.

Lincoln, his son Robert, and a small circle of advisers, bodyguards, and friends had traveled by train from Springfield, on a thirteen-day zigzag journey designed as a victory lap and last-ditch effort at building a spirit of national unity. The special train, which Mary Lincoln, Tad, and Willie caught up with in Ohio, was all decked out with American flags and red-white-and-blue bunting, and it stopped at dozens of towns and cities to allow the president-elect to show himself, shake well-wishers' hands, and deliver impassioned messages of hope and resolve. Upon crossing the border from Pennsylvania to New York State, the first stop happened to be Westfield, the hometown of Grace Bedell. On suddenly realizing this was so, Lincoln interrupted his set speech to ask if his young correspondent was in the audience. She was indeed, and when the now twelve-year-old girl reached the front of the crowd, the president-elect bent down to greet her warmly and give her a public kiss on the cheek. It was an unscripted Lincoln moment—at once disarmingly folksy and acutely me-dia-savvy—which the president-elect's allies and enemies all had a field day commenting on in their press reports.

Attempts on Lincoln's life were a constant concern, and the triumphal journey both began and ended with a terrifying scare. Not long after the train departed Springfield, a device was found on the tracks that appeared to have been placed there to cause a derailment. On the final leg of the journey, Lincoln's body-guards secretly transferred him to a series of unmarked trains that whisked him safely past Baltimore, where they had deter-mined a team of assassins lay in wait for him.

Lincoln accepted threats to his life as part and parcel of his

HARPER'S WEEKLY.

A JOURNAL OF CIVILIZATION.

VOL. V.—No. 220.]   NEW YORK, SATURDAY, MARCH 16, 1861.   [PRICE FIVE CENTS.

Entered according to Act of Congress, in the Year 1861, by Harper & Brothers, in the Clerk's Office of the District Court for the Southern District of New York.

THE INAUGURAL PROCESSION AT WASHINGTON PASSING THE GATE OF THE CAPITOL GROUNDS.—FROM A SKETCH BY OUR SPECIAL ARTIST.—[SEE PAGE 165.]

Winslow Homer's engraving of Lincoln's inaugural procession on March 4, 1861, passing the gate of the Capitol grounds.

new job, which he believed obliged him to have regular contact with ordinary people so as to know firsthand what was on their minds. For months now, Americans had been seeing Lincoln only in photographs, posters, calling cards, and prints; now they would see the man! Still, when the president-elect finally arrived at Washington's Baltimore & Ohio depot at 6 a.m. on February 23, he did so wrapped in a heavy shawl, as a passenger on a flagless and otherwise unremarkable train, the better to protect the life of the man who would soon take the helm of a bitterly divided nation.

Four months after Lincoln's inauguration, Mathew Brady and his crew headed to Bull Run, Virginia, probably arriving on July 16, 1861, together with a party of journalists and the first wave of Union Major General Irvin McDowell's 35,000-man army. The First Battle of Bull Run (also known as First Manassas) was fought five days later, on Sunday, July 21, with artillery pieces like the cannons seen in this Brady photograph playing a central role in the terrifying assaults launched by both sides. The long exposure times of Civil War–era cameras — twenty seconds or more — made action photos taken in the heat of battle an impossibility. Brady and his rivals looked instead for dramatic ways to document the preparations for combat and the death and destruction it left in its wake.

4

CITY UNDER CONSTRUCTION

In the Washington to which Lincoln returned in early 1861, lofty monuments to the republic's great and fallen heroes were still in short supply and broad swaths of the radial city's majestic plan had yet to be realized. Washington remained a chaotic patchwork of extravagantly proportioned but mud-filled avenues, imposing but half-assembled office blocks, and raw open spaces like the National Mall, which the Smithsonian's fanciful red brick Castle had all to itself except for the adjoining canal that served as a city sewer.

The colossal Treasury Building, next door to the White House, was among the vital centers of federal power, yet it was still missing its west wing. (Its basement would soon be specially fortified to serve as the president's bunker in case of a direct assault on the city.) The Supreme Court had no home of its own; neither did the Library of Congress. During the Lincoln years, both occupied space within the Capitol building.

The Washington Monument stood at less than one-third of its projected height, construction funds for it having run dry in

1854. From his second-floor White House office, the president had an all-too-perfect view of this, one of the more discouraging of all the capital's half-baked "sights." On taking office, Lincoln

On a visit to Washington, DC, in 1867, Mark Twain compared the Washington Monument with "a factory chimney with the top broken off." Construction of the gleaming 555-foot tribute to George Washington had begun on July 4, 1848, stalled from 1854 to 1877, and was finally completed in 1884. For its first five years, the monument was the world's tallest structure but was overtaken in 1889 by the Eiffel Tower, which rose to nearly twice its height in Paris.

would order the monument's sweeping grounds repurposed as a feed lot for government-owned cattle rather than let the ill-starred project go to waste entirely.

A Lincoln Timeline, 1862–1863

February 20, 1862 *Willie Lincoln, age 11, dies of typhoid fever in the White House.*

April 16, 1862 *Frees enslaved people living in Washington, DC.*

Late spring 1862 *Begins issuing military orders from the War Department telegraph office. As war intensifies and battlefield casualties mount, the search for a Union commander capable of delivering a decisive blow to the Confederate army continues in earnest.*

January 1, 1863 *Issues the Emancipation Proclamation, freeing all enslaved people living in the Confederate-held states.*

Early July 1863 *Union army victories at Gettysburg, Pennsylvania, and Vicksburg, Mississippi, mark the war's turning point.*

November 19, 1863 *Delivers the brief but memorable Gettysburg Address at the dedication of a national battlefield cemetery.*

This 1863 photograph from atop the Capitol shows Washington as still very much a work in progress. Among the "sights" captured in this panoramic view: the Botanic Garden greenhouse (1); the Smithsonian Institution's turreted castle (2) and the partly built Washington Monument behind it (3); the foul-smelling city canal (4); and the Potomac River (5).

Stray dogs and pigs roamed the city streets. Before long, so would tens of thousands of blue-jacketed Union troops assigned to defend the capital against invasion. Everywhere one turned, it seemed, Lincoln's Washington eerily mirrored the state of the nation he had come to lead—a country whose hopes and dreams stubbornly remained works in progress and whose very survival now seemed to hang by a thread.

On Inauguration Day, even the Capitol dome, "huge, grand, gloomy, ragged, and unfinished," as one visitor to the city described it, was still missing its top.

Lincoln, however, was a steady, patient man and a master of symbolism. Two years into his presidency, as the Civil War

The present-day Capitol dome replaced a much smaller one from the 1820s. Its construction, between 1857 and 1862, was a historic engineering feat that required the use of 4,454 tons of iron.

dragged on, it came to him that if he brought the construction of the Capitol dome to a swift conclusion, it might lift the nation's spirits and be read around the world as visible proof that the US government was capable of finishing whatever it started. Opponents of the president objected that surely the money might be better spent on wartime priorities. But Lincoln insisted that the dome *was* a wartime priority: "If people see the Capitol going on," he said, "it is a sign we intend the Union shall go on."

In 1952, an archivist at the National Archives discovered Lincoln's image in this photograph of the crowd massed around the speakers' platform at Gettysburg. Experts estimate this image was taken around noon, about three hours before Lincoln delivered his famously brief and memorable Gettysburg Address, on November 19, 1863.

On December 2, 1863, just two weeks after Lincoln delivered his immortal speech at Gettysburg, a giant crane hoisted the seven-and-a-half-ton bronze statue of Freedom into place atop the crown of the massive cast-iron structure. A solemn military ceremony marked the occasion, featuring a series of 35-gun salutes across the city. Lincoln himself was laid up in bed that day, apparently with smallpox, and was too ill to attend.

The next week, the 38th Congress convened under the completed dome to "face and settle" what House Speaker Schuyler Colfax called "the most important questions of the century." Chief among these was the abolition of slavery as provided for in the Thirteenth Amendment; this, Lincoln would accomplish over the next two years.

The Emancipation Proclamation

In the Emancipation Proclamation, which the White House issued on New Year's Day 1863, Lincoln redefined the North's war goals in a way meant to inspire the nation. The Union, he said, was fighting not only to put down a rebellion but to bring an end to the injustice of slavery.

The proclamation was a cleverly crafted document that did not please every slavery opponent. It immediately freed all enslaved people living within the Southern states—the states over which Lincoln then had no practical control—

but it did nothing for the time being for those living in loyal border states like Maryland and Kentucky. Lincoln's purpose in framing the proclamation in this way seems to have been to declare, in effect, that the Confederate rebels had not really founded a country of their own but were simply lawbreakers, and that he remained their president with all the power that implied.

Lincoln knew that only a constitutional amendment could end slavery once and for all. The proclamation, although largely a symbolic statement, was Lincoln's biggest step yet in that direction.

Reading the Emancipation Proclamation, an 1864 steel engraving by J. W. Watts.

5

THE ARTIST IN THE WHITE HOUSE

Both sides in the Civil War regarded the winter months of December through February as a time for their soldiers to rest and regroup. The fighting from the First Battle of Bull Run onward had been far more brutal than anyone had imagined, and by 1863, desertion had become a chronic problem for both the North and South. Cold weather often made roads impassable and no one

Union Army winter quarters at Centreville, Virginia, undated but probably late 1862 or after. Union soldiers had a better supply of tents than their Confederate counterparts and more often built log cabins like those pictured here. Poor sanitary conditions and chronic shortages of medicines made high death rates as much a reality of life in the camps as they were on the battlefield.

wished to add the extreme privations of winter warfare to the list of the soldiers' miseries and complaints.

For Lincoln, however, there was never a lull. Early in 1864, he found himself faced with a revolt from within his own cabinet when Salmon P. Chase, his treasury secretary, took steps to challenge Lincoln in the upcoming election. As the president dealt with this crisis, he also turned to the task of replacing Henry Halleck, the Union Army's disappointing commanding general—and to do so before the spring fighting began.

Busy as Lincoln was, he nonetheless agreed to a project that critics of the dome effort would surely have thought equally frivolous had their opinions been sought. The plan was for an artist, starting in February, to set up his easel in the White House and for a period of months to observe and sketch the president and his advisers, and ultimately to create a large-scale historical painting for the nation.

Francis Bicknell Carpenter, the young New York portrait painter who had proposed the idea, was well known in Washington circles, having painted three previous presidents and a handful of other government dignitaries. Skilled at navigating the Washington political and social labyrinth, he had wisely begun his quest by finding a patron willing to pay his expenses. He then talked three of the president's closest allies into putting in a good word with Lincoln for his idea: Samuel Sinclair, publisher of the *New-York Daily Tribune*; House Speaker Schuyler Colfax; and Owen Lovejoy, the representative from Illinois whom Lincoln fondly called "my best friend . . . in Congress." By one account he even persuaded Mary Lincoln to help.

On arriving in Washington on Thursday, February 4, Carpenter headed straight for the home of Owen Lovejoy, who had fallen seriously ill since their last meeting, but still wanted to write Carpenter a promised letter of introduction to his old friend. With that golden ticket in hand, Carpenter next

Artist Francis Bicknell Carpenter (1830–1900) was no stranger to Washington when he arrived there in February 1864 to undertake the project of a lifetime. Carpenter had portraits of three previous presidents, John Tyler, Millard Fillmore, and Franklin Pierce, under his belt, as well as portraits of two Lincoln Cabinet members he would now be painting again, Treasury Secretary Salmon P. Chase and Secretary of State William H. Seward.

needed to find an opportune moment to present himself to the president.

A Lincoln Timeline, 1864

February 6, 1864 *Welcomes painter Francis Bicknell Carpenter to the White House.*

February 9, 1864 *Historic photo session with Anthony Berger.*

March 10, 1864 *Promotes Ulysses S. Grant to the rank of general-in-chief of all Union forces.*

April 8, 1864 *Senate passes Thirteenth Amendment, which abolishes slavery everywhere in the United States.*

June 30, 1864 *Accepts Treasury Secretary (and would-be rival candidate) Salmon P. Chase's resignation.*

July 22, 1864 *Views Carpenter's completed painting* First Reading of the Emancipation Proclamation of President Lincoln.

November 8, 1864 *Reelected president.*

In those days, it was not all that hard to get inside the White House or even meet with the president. Every day at 8 A.M., a military guard unlocked the front door to the Executive Mansion and admitted whatever visitors had gathered in hopes of a

Military guards patrolled the White House, or Executive Mansion, as the president's residence was also known in Lincoln's time, but security was comparatively lax, and tourists were free to walk up to the front door and even meet the president if he happened to be standing in the North Portico, seen here.

presidential audience. Many came without an appointment, and some pushed and shoved their way up to the second-floor waiting rooms, where the president's three private secretaries had the last word about who got to see "the Tycoon," as they affectionately called their boss, and who did not.

On a busy morning, it could be a raucous scene and, perhaps knowing this, Carpenter opted for a different route, joining the reception line on Saturday, February 6, for the weekly afternoon open house hosted by Mary Lincoln. Carpenter's written account of his initial glimpse of Lincoln on that occasion was, in a sense, his first portrait of the president:

> *Two o'clock found me one of the throng pressing toward the centre of attraction . . . From the threshold of the "crimson" parlor . . . I had a glimpse of the gaunt figure of Mr. Lincoln in the distance, haggard-looking, dressed in black, relieved only by the prescribed white gloves; standing, it seemed to me, solitary and alone, though surrounded by the crowd, bending low now and then in the process of handshaking, and responding half abstractedly to the well-meant greetings of the miscellaneous assemblage.*

As Carpenter reached the front of the line, a White House aide whispered his name and occupation in the president's ear. He and Lincoln clasped hands and, before letting go, the president, having quickly plumbed his memory, said, "Oh yes; I know; this is the painter."

Then a merry smile crossed Lincoln's face and, looking the painter square in the eye, he raised his voice so that those around them might hear as he laid down a sort of friendly dare: "Do you think, Mr. Carpenter, that you can make a handsome picture of *me*?"

The question left the young man tongue-tied, as was doubtless its purpose, but Carpenter recovered fast enough to ask if he might speak with the president privately after the reception. Lincoln replied with a lackluster "I reckon," before moving on to the next visitor in line.

With so many people competing for the president's attention, the Lincoln White House often had a boisterous, circus-like atmosphere.

The meeting was arranged, and when Carpenter stepped inside the president's office, he found Lincoln already at his desk, deep in paperwork. The artist took a seat beside him and presented Lincoln with Owen Lovejoy's letter. Looking up from it, the president grinned broadly and said: "Well, Mr. Carpenter, we will turn you . . . loose here, and try to give you a good chance to work out your idea."

Carpenter's "idea" was for a painting far bigger in size and ambition than a standard-issue portrait. Rather, it was to be a large—bigger than life-size—history painting, the creation of which he had come to regard as a sacred mission. Carpenter was an ardent opponent of slavery and revered the president both for the steps he had already taken to bring about slavery's abolition, and those that he had pledged to take. Lincoln's most consequential act so far had come on January 1, 1863, with the release of the Emancipation Proclamation, the executive order granting freedom to all enslaved people living within the rebellious states.

Many in the North, including Lincoln himself, saw the proclamation as a turning point that redefined the Union's reason for fighting the war; some, like Carpenter, believed it was also a watershed moment in human history.

The painter's proposal was for an image recording for posterity the White House meeting in late July of 1862, at which Lincoln had first read the proclamation to the members of his cabinet and thereby set into motion a chain of events designed to lead to the end of slavery in the American republic. The painting Carpenter envisioned was one that Lincoln very much wished to see made not only for the sake of the historical record but also for the positive impact it might have on popular support for the proclamation—and the still more controversial Thirteenth Amendment to follow.

With the formalities now behind them, the president launched into a wide-ranging account of the proclamation's origins and the debate he and his cabinet officers had engaged in over its provisions. Then he walked Carpenter around the cabinet room that doubled as his office and showed him precisely where he and each of the others had been seated or standing that day.

Carpenter handed Lincoln a sketch of the scene as he had imagined it in which he had placed the president at the wrong end of the cabinet table; now, he said, he would have to start over, as his aim was for accuracy "in the cause of the truth." It was arranged for Carpenter to have the White House State Dining Room as his studio whenever it was not otherwise in use. He had hoped to live in the White House as well, but the last available bedroom had been snapped up by Robert Lincoln, the president's eldest son, who was home from Harvard. On Tuesday, February 9, Carpenter returned to the Executive Mansion with his drawing materials and got down to work.

Robert Todd Lincoln (1843–1926) was away at Harvard for much of his father's time as president but happened to be staying over at the White House when Francis Bicknell Carpenter began work on his monumental painting.

6

FEBRUARY 9: THE PRESIDENT'S MORNING

Lincoln called his second-floor office "the shop" and arrived there
every morning by 7 A.M., often—as on Tuesday, February 9—
without first bothering about breakfast. Stacks of paperwork
awaited his attention, much of it mail from people who wanted
something from him.

Ordinary citizens, political acquaintances, congressmen, military officers, and others of greater or lessser influence were among
those who wrote to him. Some were angling for a government job
or a better job than the one they already had, others for a meeting
or the chance to make history by offering their sage advice to
the president about some pressing issue of the day. A great many
simply wanted a presidential thank-you and autograph in return
for the bushel of apples or slab of venison or woolen shawl they
had sent to the White House from out of the blue.

The carriage that ferried the Lincolns around the capital was
probably the most expensive gift he received. Articles of apparel—a
smart black dress coat, a pair of socks—began arriving at such
a clip even before he had left Springfield, that Lincoln, look-

Eight sculptures representing important phases of Lincoln's life are among the many artworks that adorn the slain president's tomb in Springfield, Illinois. Fred Torrey's bronze equestrian statue depicts Lincoln as a "circuit rider" of the late 1840s and early 1850s — one of the comradely band of lawyers and court clerks who spent half the year traveling the countryside to bring prairie justice to the people of Illinois's far-flung towns and villages.

The first known photograph of Lincoln, taken in Springfield, Illinois, sometime after his election to the US House of Representatives in 1846. In a companion portrait, Lincoln's wife, Mary, looks a bit more relaxed in front of the camera than her congressman-elect husband.

Mathew Brady likely used this camera to photograph Lincoln and other notables who flocked to his New York and Washington, DC, studios during the 1860s. A subject had to stand or sit stock-still for several seconds while light poured into the dark wooden box and fixed an image on the chemically treated glass plate inside.

In November 1860, *Harper's Weekly* celebrated Lincoln's election as president with its second front-page story featuring a Lincoln portrait based on Brady's famous photograph of that year. This time, the elegantly rendered wood engraving was by an up-and-coming artist named Winslow Homer who, perhaps to differentiate his version from the earlier one, flipped the pose to have the president-elect gazing off to the left.

This fashionable black stovepipe hat, one of at least three Lincoln owned, made the six-foot-four president look even taller than he was. Lincoln added the broad silk mourning band above the brim in memory of his son Willie. He wore this hat to Ford's Theatre on the night of his murder.

Lincoln presented a chair like this one, from a set commissioned for the US House of Representatives, as a gift to Mathew Brady. The president is seen seated in the "Lincoln Chair" in Anthony Berger's February 9 photograph of Lincoln and Tad.

In October 1860, eleven-year-old Grace Bedell wrote to candidate Lincoln urging him to grow a beard if he wished to win the presidency. This elaborately decorated envelope postmarked a month later shows that Grace continued their correspondence past their initial exchange. The following February, Lincoln made a point of meeting his ardent young supporter in person during a stop on his long train journey to Washington.

This image of Lincoln on horseback in front of his Springfield home is one of many created after his death as a keepsake memorializing the slain leader. The original caption reads, "Lincoln Returns Home After His Successful Campaign for the Presidency," and dates the scene to October 1860 — a full month or more before Lincoln first sported a beard like the one in the picture.

Mary Lincoln entertained lavishly — some said *too* lavishly — throughout the Lincolns' White House years. The president himself, although he personally cared little for fancy socializing, was determined to show the world that, war or no war, life in official Washington went on as usual.

Working long hours in the White House State Dining Room, where Lincoln had invited him to set up his easel, Francis Bicknell Carpenter completed his monumental painting in six months' time. On viewing the finished canvas on July 22, 1864, the president told the artist: "It is as good a piece of work as the subject will admit of . . . and I am right glad you have done it."

On April 5, 1865, two days after Union forces captured Richmond, Lincoln, accompanied by Tad, traveled to the Confederacy's fallen capital city. Artist Lambert Hollis captured the triumphant visit in a powerful ink-and-wash drawing that underscores Lincoln's role as the Great Emancipator.

In the months and years after Lincoln's death, popular prints based in part on Anthony Berger's famous photograph of Lincoln and Tad proliferated. This hand-colored 1867 Currier & Ives lithograph purports to show the president and Tad at the White House alongside Mary Lincoln and Robert, dressed here in his army captain's uniform.

The artist who cobbled together Kelly & Sons' entry in the frenzied post-assassination keepsake competition played fast and loose with the facts. In the resulting jumbled family portrait, the boy being read to—clearly Tad—is misrepresented as Willie (who had died in 1862), with Tad depicted as the young child clinging to his mother, and Robert (who did not join the army until February 1865) posed in the background of this historically inaccurate scene.

Issued soon after Lincoln's death as demand soared for images of the martyred president, this uncut sheet of four hand-tinted lithographs based on the same 1864 Anthony Berger photograph offered customers a choice of backgrounds and formats.

Fred and Mabel Torrey collaborated on this public sculpture, titled *Lincoln and Tad*, taking their inspiration from Anthony Berger's photograph. The bronze statue was dedicated in Des Moines, Iowa, in November 1961 on the grounds of the Iowa State Capitol Building. It was paid for with funds raised primarily by Iowa's schoolchildren.

ing ahead to the coming months and years, teased the fashion-conscious Mary: "Well, wife, there is one thing likely to come of this scrape, any how [sic]. We are going to have some *new clothes!*" Two black silk stovepipe hats, which made the six-foot-four president look even more like a giant than he already did, were the gifts of rival New York hatters. When asked by a reporter which hat pleased him more, Lincoln deftly replied that he thought they "mutually surpassed each other."

Parcels delivered to the White House had to be checked for poison and explosives, and hate mail laced with vile language and hideous threats arrived daily. Lincoln rarely saw the worst of these messages, or more than a tiny fraction of the overall deluge, which reached the second floor in large canvas and leather sacks that were deposited for sorting on the desks of the president's secretaries.

Lincoln's diligent staff of three each came to the job with valuable skills. John Nicolay, the senior-most secretary, was a seasoned political operative, journalist, and trusted friend. William Stoddard likewise had a strong background in journalism. John Hay, the youngest and Lincoln's favorite, was a lawyer, a droll conversationalist who always had his ear to the ground for the latest gossip, and—what must have pleased Lincoln the most—a gifted poet. All three men were talented writers, although hardly a match for Lincoln himself. Of the letters that did reach the president's desk, Lincoln answered a surprisingly large number of them personally, dipping pen in ink and writing in the clear, unadorned cursive hand he had learned years earlier as a schoolboy.

Lincoln needed trustworthy advisers, and Joseph Holt (1807–1894) fit the bill well. A lawyer from Kentucky, Holt had persuaded that state's political leaders to remain loyal to the Union rather than join the Confederacy. He and Lincoln spent many heart-wrenching hours together deciding the fates of hundreds of soldiers who had been sentenced to death for desertion and other capital crimes.

White House visitors who arrived unbidden on February 9 were in for a disappointment. Lincoln had set the morning aside for one of his regular meetings with Judge Joseph Holt, the government lawyer charged with administering the death-penalty cases of convicted soldiers. Holt's official title was judge advocate general of the United States Army, and it was his job to ensure that justice was done. As the war dragged on, fresh army volunteers had become harder to find, and the draftees who took their place often lacked a deep-seated commitment to the Union. As desertion numbers mounted, Lincoln felt torn: He wished to be merciful, but he needed the army to do its duty. Lincoln relied on Holt, a smart, precise, no-nonsense Kentuckian, to help him strike the right balance.

As Francis Carpenter sat sketching in a corner, Holt and Lincoln huddled together at the cabinet table and methodically went down the day's list. On some days, there might be thirty cases to consider; on others, as many as one hundred. Lincoln took no pleasure in playing God, and whenever possible latched onto any reasonable excuse—the youth of the condemned man, a question about the state of his mental health, the lack of a prior record of lawbreaking—to tip the scales of justice toward mercy. On the days when he spared a soldier's life, he once said, "I go to bed happy as I think how joyous the signing of my name will make him and his family and his friends." The order Lincoln signed in such cases hardly sounded like the fateful decree it was: "Let this man take the oath of Dec. 8 [i.e., the 1863 Oath of Allegiance to the United States] and be discharged."

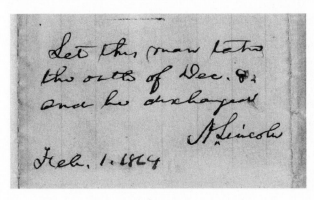

A tersely worded presidential order like this one spelled the difference between life and death for a soldier found guilty of desertion.

The most notorious prisoner discussed on February 9 was Confederate major Edgar A. Burroughs, a one-time Methodist minister who had raised a regiment of guerrilla fighters in

Princess Anne County, Virginia, and "wreaked havoc" on the occupying Union force. Found guilty at trial, Burroughs had been sentenced to death by hanging.

Lincoln was somehow already aware the major was in poor health and found himself leaning in Burroughs's favor. Before he could act, however, Holt chimed in about a new development in the case. Major Burroughs, it seems, had recently taken part in a failed prison break attempt and been shot dead by the sentry on duty.

On hearing the news, Lincoln said ruefully: "I ought to be obliged to him for taking his fate in his own hands; he has saved *me* a deal of trouble."

When the mantelpiece clock sounded the noon hour, Lincoln pushed back from his place at the table and, extending his long, gangly arms like wings to signal an end, said in his cracked, shrill voice, "I guess we will go no further with these cases to-day."

Judge Holt then departed to make way for the cabinet session that was about to start. Lincoln had invited Carpenter to stay for this next meeting as well. As the cabinet members shuffled into the president's study, Lincoln remarked to the painter with amusement that he had still not had his breakfast; now there would be no time for lunch. Once the president's advisers had taken their places, he introduced Carpenter and explained that they were all to appear together in one of his paintings. He asked the secretaries for their cooperation. Then, in his canny, even-handed way, Lincoln launched into a meandering story

Lincoln chose strong, ambitious leaders to serve in his cabinet, including some who wanted his job for themselves. Pictured here from left to right: Edward Bates (attorney general), Gideon Welles (Navy), Montgomery Blair (postmaster general), William H. Seward (State), Salmon P. Chase (Treasury), the president, General Winfield Scott (visiting, not a cabinet member), Caleb B. Smith (Interior), Simon Cameron (War).

meant to reassure his cabinet secretaries that he had their own best interests at heart every bit as much as he did Carpenter's.

The story concerned another artist of some note, a sculptor named Thomas D. Jones, who, like Carpenter, had plied his trade among Washington's dignitaries but, by failing to mind the clock, had managed to wear out his welcome with one of them. The author of Jones's undoing, Lincoln explained over his own laughter, had been none other than the Union Army's highest-ranking officer at the time, General Winfield Scott, also known as "Old Fuss and Feathers" for his flamboyant taste in military headgear. Jones had held the general in captivity through several sittings before Scott, who was more used to giving orders than to taking them, had simply gotten up from his chair one day, declared the sculpture done, and left.

Might Carpenter suffer the same fate? He was determined not to do so, and as a precaution had set up a photo session for the president that very afternoon at Mathew Brady's Washington studio. One great advantage of photography over painting was that it was quick. A photographic portrait taken at 3 P.M. could be wrapped and ready to go later that same day. Photos for study would give Carpenter another means to observe the president from various angles and distances while also saving the latter precious time. Might such special photographs be put to other uses as well? The thought would surely have crossed Lincoln's and Carpenter's minds, and Mathew Brady's, too.

In 1858, Brady had boldly expanded his business by opening an opulent Washington studio to complement his thriving New York establishment. He called the new venture Brady's National Photographic Art Gallery, a puffed-up version of the Broadway studio name. A "national" studio—he sometimes dropped that grand word from ads—made it sound even more like a cultural institution rather than a money-making venture. In reality it was both things, and for years afterward Brady's gallery would remain one of the capital city's top tourist attractions: the destination of choice for anyone wishing to view an art exhibition— or to have their picture taken or to stock up on souvenir photos of the great and powerful.

Brady's occupied the three upper floors of a pair of adjacent four-story buildings along a bustling stretch of Pennsylvania Avenue, the capital's only paved road. Ascending from the ground level, visitors came to the second-floor public gallery—an elegant parlor-like space with an ample selection on view of Brady's "startling likenesses of the great," as he immodestly called his portraits of illustrious Americans.

Tourists flocked to the gallery to stand eye to eye with former presidents, Union generals, members of Congress and the Supreme Court, famous authors, artists, stage performers, and inventors. Brady regarded his portrait collection as his personal tribute to the nation and invited all comers, free of charge, to gorge themselves on the richness of his achievement.

He hoped, of course, that some in the crowd would proceed upstairs, past the third-floor work area, to the skylit "operating room," on four, where paying customers could have their own portraits made, perhaps even by the same "operator" who had immortalized the likeness of General Grant or Alexander Graham Bell or the president himself. It was certainly flattering to think so. Most people looked upon the act of sitting for a costly, high-end photographic portrait as a once-in-a-lifetime affair, a formal occasion that called for dressing up in one's Sunday best as surely as did any wedding or funeral. To have such a sitting in Brady's celebrated shrine made the special occasion seem all the more memorable.

Customers could choose from an elaborate menu of options. The largest format measured 17" x 20", was printed on luxuriously

A dramatic carte de visite made from a portrait taken at Brady's Washington studio. The subject is thought to be the wife of Union Army Major General George Vickers. Of the Vickers' four sons, one fought for the Union and one for the Confederacy. The latter died of his wounds at the Battle of Shiloh.

thick, textured paper, and came with a whopping price tag in the hundreds of dollars. Brady, with his flamboyant, carnival-barker flair for promotion, had dreamed up a suitably grand name for this top-of-the-line offering: the "Imperial." An Imperial portrait might be further enhanced by the addition of hand-colored highlights applied by an artist. A portrait with these finishing touches had extra special cachet: yes, it was a photograph, but it was a painting, too!

At the other extreme were the ubiquitous, palm-size cartes de visite that measured 4 1/2" x 2 1/2" and sold for as little as twenty-five cents apiece. Brady did a brisk business, both in the cards he made for ordinary customers and those he offered for sale of the collectible variety. In the new age of photographic mass reproduction, Brady and his rivals all felt entitled to profit freely from the images of the famous subjects they photographed, and even Lincoln, who knew the law better than most, seems to have acknowledged as much when he wrote an acquaintance that he had no control over Brady's pictures of him. As in the case of the New York hatters, Lincoln was more concerned about not showing favoritism to one photographer over another. One year earlier, when Mathew Brady's longtime assistant Alexander Gardner resigned to open his own rival Washington studio, Lincoln promised Gardner to be his first customer and proved to be as good as his word.

7

FEBRUARY 9:
THE PRESIDENT'S AFTERNOON

At 3 P.M., accompanied by Carpenter, Lincoln headed down-
stairs to the north entrance of the Executive Mansion and waited
on the portico steps for the carriage that was to take them for the
mile-long ride to Brady's. As the two men stood chatting, an aide
rushed out to hand the president an urgent message. On looking
up from the paper, Lincoln observed a family of tourists shyly
approaching him along the semicircular carriageway, which in
those days was completely accessible to the public. Soon hands
were being shaken and Lincoln was bending down to greet each
of the awestruck couple's shy little boys. Responding to the president's down-to-earth and fatherly manner, the children's own
father exclaimed, "The Lord is with you, Mr. President. The Lord
and the people too, sir; and the people too!"

The presidential carriage had still not arrived and, rather
than wait any longer, Lincoln proposed to Carpenter that they
walk. On the way to the photo gallery, the president regaled the

painter with stories about other high government officials whose physical appearance, like his own, fell short of their admirers' expectations.

He recalled the time when, during a visit by Daniel Webster to Springfield, a crowd had gathered to catch a glimpse of the Great Orator, as Webster was known. The commotion sparked the curiosity of a child who had happened by, and to whom a bystander was pleased to explain that "the biggest man in the world" was about to pass in the street. The boy apparently took this to mean that some sort of circus performer had come to town. All was excitement until the Massachusetts senator finally showed himself. According to Lincoln, the child, naming a certain well-known, barrel-chested local character, groaned his disappointment, "But laws, he ain't half as big as old G!"

Brady's Battlefield Photographs

Brady rarely spent much time in Washington and, his eyesight having begun to fail him, did not get behind a camera much anymore, either. When not peacocking about New York to drum up business for his Manhattan gallery, he and the members of a small, hand-picked field crew roamed the countryside from Pennsylvania southward, a portable darkroom in tow, to create what he envisioned as an epic documentary history of the war.

Brady photographers recorded panoramic views of one battlefield after another, often arriving on the scene only a day or two after the shooting had stopped and before the dead had been removed for burial. They visited the Union Army's advance positions as well, making portraits of the soldiers and their commanding officers and photographing vignettes of their rugged camp life.

Mathew Brady (second from right) and his camera crew in the field in Berlin, Maryland, 1862.

The Civil War, with all the forced separations it occasioned, had been very good for Brady's business as it became the custom for soldiers to carry photos of their loved ones into battle as talismans and reminders of better times, and to mail photos of themselves back home to those who anxiously awaited their return. Brady had never shied away from touting photography's unique power to draw the viewer into an intimate, face-to-face communion with a subject beyond one's immediate reach. In wartime, he became shameless in this regard, in one none-too-subtle ad reminding readers of the *New-York Herald*: "You cannot tell how soon it may be too late."

By 1864, Brady was as much a man on a mission as Francis Carpenter, and he had come to rely on a handful of trusted managers to oversee both his studios. The manager who welcomed the president and Carpenter on February 9 was a German emigré painter turned photographer named Anthony Berger.

Brady and Berger had likely first met in New York a decade earlier when the latter rented space in the same building where the famous photographer had his gallery. Brady always needed artists to do his deluxe finishing work. Berger may have joined the gallery staff in this role and then learned about cameras and moved up the Brady ladder. For an artist on the rise, that Broadway building was evidently the place to be: Among the other painters with studios at the same Broadway address just then was none other than Francis Carpenter. The photographer Carpenter later chose for the all-important February 9 assignment may well have been an old acquaintance of his, and perhaps even a friend.

Photographers called themselves "operators" and the portion of the studio where they performed their magic the "operating room." In some ways, the latter resembled a theater with a stage-like space in which the sitter posed before a curtain or other scenic backdrop and a backstage area where a supply of furnishings and props—a globe, an assortment of books, a decorative rug—stood ready for use in creating the desired effect. Because sitters were required to hold still for a period of several seconds, the right prop might also serve to relax or steady the client: a fluted pedestal to rest one's hand or elbow on while striking a commanding or contemplative pose, a well-proportioned chair to settle into comfortably.

Mathew Brady was such a publicity hound that he even managed to make one of his studio chairs famous: the carved oak armchair that appears in a great many of the Washington studio's pictures. This was the "Lincoln Chair," known as such because Brady had received it as a gift from the president himself—a thank-you, perhaps, for the huge boost Brady's first portrait of Lincoln, taken in New York on the day of the Cooper Union address, had given his chances for the presidency, or perhaps for more mundane reasons. Not every chair suited the long-legged president and when Lincoln came across this one, he may have reasoned that Brady's studio was a good home for it, knowing he would be visiting there from time to time, and not wanting the photographs made of him to suffer on account of the seating arrangements.

Some time that afternoon, Tad Lincoln, the president's youngest son, arrived at Brady's, presumably by carriage, escorted by Mary Lincoln. He was beautifully dressed in a black suit that buttoned all the way up in the front, and with a gold watch chain that resembled his father's.

The Lincoln Chair

Exactly how Lincoln came by the chair is not known, but it was one of a set of 262 leather upholstered armchairs and desks made in 1857 for the US House of Representatives. House membership at the time stood at 237, leaving twenty-five extras to be put in storage or to other use. Lincoln had once served a single term in the House—his highest previous elective office. His good friend House Speaker Schuyler Colfax may have decided he should have the chair as a souvenir. Four later presidents posed seated in it too, as did senators, Supreme Court justices, Walt Whitman, and Mark Twain. (See color insert for a photograph of another chair from the same set.)

Several photographs of the president were taken. As the session was winding down, Carpenter and Berger—perhaps with some coaxing from Mary Lincoln—prepared for one final picture, a more intimate pose in which Tad would take part. The president—in his favorite chair—would be seated in profile facing right, with Tad standing by his left arm. Berger handed

Lincoln a large, leather-bound volume and asked him to balance it, open, on his crossed left leg to give the impression that he was reading to his son. The president, who often did read to Tad at bedtime, must have liked the idea well enough because he obliged Berger further by putting on his reading glasses—a personal touch not seen before or afterward in any of Lincoln's photographs.

As Tad's father pretended to be reading to him, Tad pretended to listen, his gaze fixed on the massive book that viewers afterward assumed must be the Lincoln family Bible. In fact, it was a Brady studio sample catalogue. The chronically restless and mischievous Tad managed to hold still long enough for the exposure to be made—and immortalized. Perhaps the president had slipped the boy a coin in exchange for his cooperation. It would not have been the first time.

Ten-year-old Thomas—Tadpole—Lincoln was the family's fourth and youngest child. He bore the name of the president's father, notwithstanding the cruelty the president had suffered as a child at Thomas Lincoln's hands. Lincoln, having had three previous chances to do so, had held off paying his father the tribute of perpetuating his name for as long as possible. His fourth son's exceptionally large head at birth had reminded him of a tadpole's, and the affectionate nickname Tad stuck in part because Lincoln still could not bear to speak his own father's given name.

Although best known to White House visitors and staff for his colorful high jinks, Tad was a troubled young child who had already experienced extraordinary suffering. Just two years earlier, his older brother and best friend Willie had died in the White House of typhoid fever. From their earliest Springfield days, the two boys had been inseparable companions; then, suddenly, Willie was gone. Tad caught the fever himself and might well have died that winter, too. There was hardly time to celebrate his recovery, however, and his parents' grief over the loss of Willie vastly compounded his own, their downward-spiraling depression having left them—Mary Lincoln especially—ill equipped to attend to his needs. After Willie's death, the First Lady disappeared into her bedroom for three or more weeks. The president resumed his schedule but repeatedly visited the vault in which his son's casket had been placed and the White House room in which he had died. From then onward, the president went everywhere, often with Tad at his side, wearing a broad black mourning band wrapped around his hat.

Daunting challenges had dogged Tad from the beginning. Willie had always been the Lincolns' golden boy: smart, quick, well-spoken, and generous of spirit like his father; Tad was the family's wounded bird. Some difficulty for which no name yet existed kept Tad from concentrating on his lessons and at age ten he had still not learned to read. Making matters worse, the cleft palate with which he was born garbled his speech and rendered ordinary conversation a terrible strain. When Tad spoke, only those closest to him could tell what he was saying.

The president's way of handling all this was to lavish his son with toys and attention, just the opposite of what his own father would have done. Allowing Tad to run riot through the Executive Mansion, Lincoln issued only the mildest of rebukes even when the boy burst into a cabinet session or meeting of his generals.

For their part, the White House staff took a shine to the Lincolns' impetuous merry prankster, who had once held a yard sale on the White House lawn of items culled from his parents' wardrobe and driven a chair harnessed to a pair of goats through an East Room reception hosted by the First Lady. The military guards assigned to the president let Tad join them at meals, and when the Lincolns outfitted their son with a custom-tailored officer's uniform complete with white dress gloves and ceremonial sword, the guards delighted in awarding him the imaginary rank of "third lieutenant."

In October of 1863, after the president issued the order that made Thanksgiving a national holiday, Tad, slyly mimicking the pardon seekers who daily laid siege outside the president's office, begged his father to spare the life of the turkey a well-wisher had sent the family for their Christmas dinner. Lincoln obliged, granting a reprieve to Jack the Turkey—Tad's name for the bird he had already trained to follow him everywhere—although Jack's good luck ran out a year later.

Following the February 9 photo session at Brady's, the Lincolns returned by carriage to the White House to prepare

Tad posed for his own carte de visite photograph in his spiffy "third lieutenant's" uniform, which he delighted in wearing when accompanying his father to review the troops and on other special occasions.

for the weekly Tuesday levee, or evening reception, for which the president would once again don his white gloves and, with the First Lady by his side, greet throngs of visitors. Lincoln disliked these occasions, but the day had already been a productive one and, all in all, a happy one as well. In the Lincoln White House good times rarely lasted for long, however, and the following evening, at 8:30 P.M., after another long day of reviewing execution orders, an alarm sounded on the Executive Mansion grounds, signaling that a fire had broken out in the president's stables.

Unnerved by the mysterious fire that destroyed the White House stables, Lincoln ordered that the structure be immediately rebuilt, as if to erase the memory of the terrible evening when his horse and Tad's two ponies were among the animals killed.

Lincoln himself raced across the lawn to help save the horses and had to be held back from entering the building, which was already engulfed in flames. Reporting the incident to John Hay, who had left the president's staff a month earlier to serve in the army, the senior secretary John Nicolay wrote: "The carriages & coupé alone were saved—everything else went—six horses, including the President's, ours, and Tad's two ponies, are 'gone where the good horses go.' Tad," Nicolay continued, "was in bitter tears at the loss of his ponies, and his heaviest grief was his recollection that one of them had belonged to Willie."

Earlier that day, Mary Lincoln had dismissed her coachman—quite possibly for having failed to show up on time the previous afternoon for the trip to Brady's—and Robert Lincoln, who was home from college, suspected it was he who had torched the stables in revenge. Others feared even worse: that the fire had been set as part of a failed attempt to lure the president within range of an assassin's rifle.

This Anthony Berger photograph of Lincoln in his office was among those taken during Lincoln's only White House photo session. It was made on April 26, 1864, the day that a very irritable Tad tried to stop Berger's assistants from getting at their equipment. Perhaps in reaction to Tad, Lincoln turned his head during the exposure, causing his face to blur.

8

IMAGES ON THE MARCH

Carpenter remained a shadow White House presence through late July of 1864. He could often be found, sketchbook in hand, seated off to one side in the president's office. If a visitor, puzzled by the sight of a stranger who was clearly not engaged in the president's business, asked for an explanation, Lincoln would shrug good-naturedly and reply: "Oh, you need not mind him; he is but a painter."

That spring, Carpenter arranged two more photo sessions with Anthony Berger: the first at the Brady studio on April 20 and the second, just six days later, in the president's office, the only time Lincoln was ever photographed at the White House.

Tad, unhappy to have the spotlight turned away from him even briefly, interrupted the latter sitting by causing a commotion when assistants accompanying Berger turned a room Tad claimed as his territory into a temporary darkroom, and the now eleven-year-old boy angrily locked them out and refused to surrender the key.

Lincoln rarely slept more than a few hours a night and allowed himself few breaks during his long, demanding days.

Apart from an impromptu visit from Tad, hardly anyone or any-thing had the power to distract him; by 1864, he had given up the daily afternoon carriage rides with Mary Lincoln that his wife had urged upon him, early in his term, for his own well-being.

Bringing an end to the war had become his all-consuming obsession. Carpenter would later recall watching Lincoln day after day as he labored at his desk:

"Absorbed in his papers, he would become unconscious of my presence, while I intently studied every line and shade of expression in that furrowed face. In repose, it was the saddest face I ever knew. There were days when I could scarcely look into it without crying."

Often awake in the middle of the night, the president would stride across the White House grounds to the War Department and on up to the second-floor telegraph office to read the latest incoming battlefield dispatches, transmit orders, and chat with the soldiers on duty. From there, he might go for a late-night walk around the city, sometimes alone and sometimes, during the early months of 1864, with Francis Carpenter at his side.

Carpenter's six months at the White House had been a most eventful time for the president. Lincoln had dismissed the army's commanding officer and appointed General Ulysses S. Grant to lead all Union forces fighting the Confederacy. By doing so, he had laid the groundwork for the North's final victory. To help ensure Grant's success, he had issued a call for 500,000 additional army volunteers.

Lincoln had also watched with amusement as Treasury Secretary Salmon P. Chase's clumsy attempt to snatch the Republican nomination away from him unraveled, as he had known it would. And he had grown increasingly confident about his reelection that fall and was looking ahead to seeing the end of the war and to playing a part in the post-war reunification of the republic.

Carpenter completed his monumental painting in midsummer (see color insert). It measured nine feet by fourteen and a half feet, or nearly twice the height and length of a full-grown horse. On July 22, the artist asked the president and his cabinet to join him in the State Dining Room for a viewing.

By the time Carpenter finished his grand painting of the president and his cabinet in July of 1864, Treasury Secretary Salmon P. Chase (second from left) had resigned, having recently made a blundering attempt to replace Lincoln as the Republicans' presidential nominee for that year. This print, based on the painting, first went on sale in 1866.

The president was pleased with the result. After acknowledging he was no art critic, Lincoln, speaking for the group, gave Carpenter's painting his blessing, saying, "In my judgement, it is as good a piece of work as the subject will admit of . . . and I am right glad you have done it!" He then ordered that it be put on public view in the East Room.

More showings followed. In March of 1865, during the time of Lincoln's second inaugural celebration, *First Reading of the Emancipation Proclamation of President Lincoln*, as Carpenter's painting had come to be known, moved to the Capitol Rotunda where thousands more filed past it appreciatively. It then embarked on a national tour. Carpenter lobbied Congress to purchase the work as a permanent tribute to one of American history's noblest episodes, but he failed to generate support for the expenditure. More than a decade would pass before a wealthy New York patron finally agreed to buy the painting as a gift to the nation.

A Lincoln Timeline, 1865

January 31, 1865 *House of Representatives passes Thirteenth Amendment.*

March 4, 1865 *In second inaugural address, Lincoln promises a post-war national reunification "with malice toward none, with charity for all."*

April 9, 1865 *Confederate General Robert E. Lee surrenders at Appomattox Courthouse, Virginia, ending the Civil War.*

April 14, 1865 *President Lincoln assassinated at Ford's Theatre, Washington, DC.*

In the meantime, the nimble artist looked for other ways to profit from his work. He arranged for a black-and-white print to be issued based on it, to be sold in large quantities as a patriotic collectible. A small number of deluxe printer's proofs, signed by the artist, were also to be put on sale. As a friendly gesture, Lincoln placed his own name at the top of the list of those wishing to reserve one of these special copies. The project was delayed, however, and the president did not live long enough to receive his purchase.

The Brady gallery soon had photographic prints on offer from the latest batch of Lincoln portraits. Not included among them, however, was the February 9 portrait of Lincoln and Tad. No one knows for sure why not, but two explanations are plausible. Carpenter may have already had in mind the special use to which he later put the tender father-son image—as the central element in a Lincoln family portrait—and asked the studio to keep it out of public view in the meantime. Or Lincoln himself may have wanted the picture withheld out of concern that viewers might mistakenly believe the book in the photograph was a Bible, which it certainly did resemble and which some later viewers did indeed assume was the Good Book.

Photo historians look back on President Lincoln's visit to Brady's on February 9, 1864 as a magical moment. The photographs made that day have been reproduced, repurposed, and re-imagined beyond all reckoning. Of the six portraits Berger made, all remain well-known and four rank among the most studied and viewed images of any notable American.

In 1909, the photograph known as the Famous Profile served as the model for the portrait embossed on the Lincoln penny. In 1928, the photograph that Robert Lincoln later called the Most Satisfactory Likeness was made into the portrait engraved on the five-dollar bill. When a new design for the bill went into circulation in 2008, it bore a portrait image adapted from another of the six February 9 photographs.

Lincoln's image has appeared on two versions of the five-dollar bill: the original 1928 bank note and the present-day one first released in 2008. Both portraits were based on Berger photos from February 9, 1864.

The US Mint introduced the Lincoln penny in 1909 to mark the one hundredth anniversary of Abraham Lincoln's birth. Its likeness was based on the so-called Famous Profile, another of the photos taken by Anthony Berger on February 9, 1864, as adapted by sculptor Victor David Brenner, a Lithuanian Jewish immigrant.

9

AFTERGLOW

The assassination of Abraham Lincoln on April 14, 1865, just five days after the Confederate surrender at Appomattox Courthouse that ended the Civil War, plunged millions of Americans into mourning and created intense demand for images of the slain president. Sales of Lincoln photographs, prints, mourning ribbons, and other keepsakes and paraphernalia—including hastily put-together images of the presidential deathbed scene—skyrocketed. Large crowds turned out to view the president's casket at ceremonial stops in city after city as it solemnly made its way by train to Springfield along a circuitous route that largely reprised in reverse Lincoln's 1861 journey to Washington. The body of young Willie Lincoln had been exhumed and his casket placed on the same train for joint burial in the Illinois capital on May 4.

Newspapers and magazines were awash with memorial tributes and illustrations. *Harper's Weekly* gave over its entire May 6 issue to the president's murder, funeral, and martyrdom. *Harper's* needed an attention-grabbing cover image and arranged with

The locomotive that pulled the special nine-car train carrying the bodies of Lincoln and his son Willie from Washington to Springfield. In all, the train passed through 180 cities, stopping in ten of them for memorial processions and viewings attended by millions.

Mathew Brady to publish an engraving based on the still-unknown photo of Lincoln and Tad. The understated (and inaccurate) caption read: "President Lincoln at home." It must have reduced a great many readers to tears.

Later that same year, Francis Carpenter did indeed paint a Lincoln family portrait, a tableau pieced together from the Berger image of the president and Tad and other photos provided by Mary Lincoln. Carpenter chose to portray the Lincolns in 1861, a time of great promise for them all that allowed him to include Willie. He limited his palette to blacks and grays with a view to speeding the production of the black-and-white print version he

THE REISSUE OF

HARPER'S WEEKLY.

JOURNAL OF CIVILIZATION.

VOL. IX.—No. 436.]　　　　NEW YORK, SATURDAY, MAY 6, 1865.　　　　[SINGLE COPIES TEN CENTS.
[$4.00 PER YEAR IN ADVANCE.

Entered according to Act of Congress, in the Year 1865, by Harper & Brothers, in the Clerk's Office of the District Court for the Southern District of New York.

PRESIDENT LINCOLN AT HOME.—[PHOTOGRAPHED BY BRADY.]

The world first saw the Lincoln-and-Tad image as the wood-engraved cover illustration of *Harper's Weekly* for May 6, 1865, the issue that reported on Lincoln's funeral.

was keen to get on the market while the demand for Lincoln images remained high. By then, Carpenter had also written the first of several articles about his time in the Lincoln White House.

Before the mournful year of 1865 was over, Francis Carpenter painted this Lincoln family portrait, inserting a flopped version of Anthony Berger's Lincoln-and-Tad photograph within a scene for which Mary Lincoln lent him photos of her other children. Carpenter chose to depict the Lincolns in 1861, when Willie was still alive and Robert had not yet joined the army.

In 1866, he gathered his recollections in a book that enjoyed a huge sale. He continued to paint for many years afterward but was largely forgotten by the time of his death in 1900. Carpenter's *First Reading* was eventually hung in a Senate stairwell of the US Capitol Building and remains there today.

A Lincoln Timeline, 1865 to Present

1866 *US Post Office Department issues a 15-cent Lincoln memorial stamp, the first of dozens honoring the sixteenth president over the years.*

1868 *First statue of Lincoln erected in front of Washington, DC, City Hall.*

1871 *Tad Lincoln, age 18, dies in Chicago, of pneumonia or tuberculosis.*

1909 *On the one-hundredth anniversary of his birth, Lincoln is depicted in profile on the copper penny.*

1914 *Featured on the five-dollar bill.*

1922 *Lincoln Memorial dedicated in Washington, DC.*

1926 *Robert Lincoln dies in Vermont at age 83.*

1941 *Mount Rushmore National Memorial, with monumental sculpted heads of Lincoln, Washington, Jefferson, and Theodore Roosevelt, completed in southwestern South Dakota.*

1984 *The US Postal Service's "A Nation of Readers" stamp, based on the Anthony Berger photograph of Lincoln and Tad, issued.*

2012 *Historians estimate that 15,000 books have been written about Lincoln.*

2015 *States with the most streets named "Lincoln": Illinois (344), Ohio (214), New Jersey (131).*

The image of Lincoln reading to Tad spread rapidly in an endless array of prints and adaptations and played an important part in defining the slain president's legacy. As a depiction of his fatherly side, it touched viewers by underscoring his loving nature and basic humanity. By showing him as he pored over a book, it reminded viewers of the extraordinary power of his words and provided a timeless comment on the power of books to bind generations together. To those who saw in the image a picture of a father reading the Bible to his son, it bolstered the

This Currier and Ives print titled "President Lincoln at Home: Reading the Scriptures to His Wife and Son" from 1865 inserted Mary into the scene and helped spread the false notion that the book Lincoln is shown holding was a Bible.

In this carte de visite photograph made from an 1865 painting by F. B. Schell, a framed picture of the late Willie Lincoln hangs on the wall, upper right.

extravagant claims made after his death that Lincoln had lived a spiritually pure, Christ-like life and had now surely joined George Washington in heaven. Even in death, Lincoln remained a hated figure to a minority of Americans—not all of them Southerners—whose lives and livelihoods revolved around the institution of slavery and who cursed him for having in effect destroyed their world. But for everyone else, Lincoln the man swiftly morphed into Lincoln the hero and Lincoln the saint—the great yet also humble president who even in wartime had taken time out to read to his son.

Mathew Brady and the photographers he trained produced an astonishing body of work, distinguishing themselves as pioneers both of photographic portraiture and wartime pictorial journalism. Brady felt sure Congress would purchase his great Civil War photographic archive on behalf of the nation; but like Francis Carpenter, he too was disappointed when Congress declined his offer. Having allowed his expenses to run away from him during the war years, Brady was never able to regain his professional footing afterward. He died deep in debt in 1896.

In 1865, Anthony Berger left his job at the Brady gallery and returned to New York, opening a photographic studio in downtown Brooklyn. Among the first images he offered for sale was his February 9 photograph of Lincoln and Tad, altered slightly by him in order to be able to claim it as his own work under the law. Brady, of course, sold prints of the exceptionally popular image too, as did photographers in Philadelphia, Chicago, and

A notice in the *Brooklyn Eagle* for May 9, 1865, announces the opening in downtown Brooklyn of a photographic studio by Anthony Berger, creator of the image of Abraham Lincoln reading "the Bible" to his son, here misidentified as Willie.

probably elsewhere, who had simply gotten hold of a copy of the image and photographed the photograph, thereby creating a new negative from which to (illegally) print and sell as many copies as the market would bear. Berger appears to have continued working at least through the 1870s. What happened to him after that is not known. It is a sad irony that no photographic portrait of this gifted "operator" is believed to exist.

Following his father's death, Tad Lincoln went to live in Chicago with Mary Lincoln and his older brother Robert and traveled widely with his mother in Europe. He never overcame his learning difficulties and in 1871 died of pneumonia or tuberculosis at the age of eighteen.

Mary Lincoln died in 1882 having struggled terribly with depression and grief following the deaths of Willie, the president, and Tad, and by some accounts having grown emotionally unstable under the weight of her misfortunes.

Robert Lincoln was the only one of the Lincolns' four children to survive into adulthood. He graduated from Harvard, grew a beard, became a successful lawyer and businessman, and served

In this 1905 portrait, Robert Todd Lincoln looks very much like the prosperous lawyer and businessman he became. Although he held two high-level government posts during his long working life, he generally avoided the limelight and was most famous simply for being Abraham Lincoln's son. The Lincoln Sea, a cold stretch of the Arctic Ocean between Greenland and Canada, is named for him.

his country as Secretary of War in the Garfield administration and ambassador to Great Britain under Benjamin Harrison. As the sole remaining heir of the much beloved Abraham Lincoln, it was often said of Robert that the presidency of the United States was his for the asking. Robert never asked. He and his father had never gotten along and had rarely wanted or even liked the same things. Robert was a pert, impatient, humorless man who, like his mother, craved luxury and all the other trappings of wealth and position. He recalled bitterly once that during the years of his Springfield childhood, his father—so generous to and adored by others—had not been home for him nearly enough. As a circuit lawyer, Abraham Lincoln had indeed been obliged to travel for half the year from courthouse to courthouse in various localities around the state. As his career blossomed, he may well have been happiest when matching wits with his rivals before a judge and a roomful of spectators. For his son Robert, those early years—so ripe with promise for the future president—had boiled down to a single, melancholy childhood memory: the image of a man packing his saddlebags, heading out the door, and vanishing into the distance—a lone rider on horseback bound for the Illinois woods.

Lincoln's gold watch was purchased in the 1850s from a Springfield, Illinois, jeweler. Its distinctive chain can be glimpsed in the portrait of Lincoln reading to his son Tad and other photographs taken by Anthony Berger on February 9, 1864.

BIBLIOGRAPHY

Anderson, David D, editor. *The Literary Works of Abraham Lincoln*. Columbus, OH: Charles E. Merrill, 1970.

Burlingame, Michael, editor. *With Lincoln in the White House: Letters, Memoranda, and Other Writings of John G. Nicolay, 1860–1865*. Carbondale and Edwardsville: Southern Illinois UP, 2000.

———— and John R. Turner Ettlinger, editors. *Inside Lincoln's White House: The Complete Civil War Diary of John Hay*. Carbondale and Edwardsville: Southern Illinois UP, 1997.

Carpenter, Francis Bicknell. *Six Months at the White House with Abraham Lincoln: The Story of a Picture*. Introduction by Harold Holzer. Washington, DC: White House Historical Association, 2008.

Cornelius, Judson K., *Political Humour*. Mumbai: Better Yourself Books, 2001.

Crain, Caleb. "How Soon It May Be Too Late," *New York Times Book Review* (April 2, 2013), p. 11.

Eaton, John. *Grant, Lincoln and the Freedmen: Reminiscences of the Civil War*. New York: Longmans, Green, and Co., 1907.

Epstein, Daniel Mark. *Lincoln's Men: The President and His Private Secretaries*. Washington, DC, Smithsonian Books, 2009.

Fox, Richard Wightman. *Lincoln's Body: A Cultural History*. New York: W.W. Norton, 2015.

Goodwin, Doris Kearns. *Team of Rivals: The Political Genius of Abraham Lincoln*. New York: Simon and Schuster, 2005.

Hamilton, Charles and Lloyd Ostendorf. *Lincoln in Photographs: An Album of Every Known Pose*. Norman, OK: University of Oklahoma UP, 1963.

Hazelton, George Cochrane. *The National Capitol: Its Architecture, Art and History*. New York: J. F. Taylor, 1907.

Heberton, Craig. "Chewing on A. Berger," *Abraham Lincoln at Gettysburg* blog: https://abrahamlincolnatgettysburg.wordpress.com/2014/02/22/chewing-on-a-berger-part-i/

————. "February 9, 1864: Lincoln's Magical Photographic Session with Anthony Berger," *Abraham Lincoln at Gettysburg* blog: https://abrahamlincolnatgettysburg.wordpress.com/2015/02/10/february-9–1864-lincolns-magical-photographic-session-with-anthony-berger/

Holzer, Harold, editor. *Dear Mr. Lincoln: Letters to the President*. Boston: Da Capo Press, 1993.

————. *Father Abraham: Lincoln and His Sons*. Honesdale, PA: Calkins Creek, 2011.

————. *Lincoln and the Power of the Press*. New York: Simon and Schuster, 2014.

————. *Lincoln President-Elect: Abraham Lincoln and the Great Succession Winter, 1860–1861*. New York: Simon and Schuster, 2009.

————, Gabor S. Boritt, and Mark E. Neely, Jr. *The Lincoln Image: Abraham Lincoln and the Popular Print*. New York: Scribner, 1984.

King, Gilbert. "The History of Pardoning Turkeys Began with Tad Lincoln." *Smithsonian Magazine* online, posted November 21, 2012: www.smithsonianmag.com/history/the-history-of-pardoning-turkeys-began-with-tad-lincoln-141137570/

Kunhardt, Peter W., Jr., editor. *The Photographs of Abraham Lincoln*. Essays by Harold Holzer and Philip B. Kunhardt III. Göttingen and New York: Steidl and Meserve-Kunhardt Foundation, 2015.

Lehrman Institute. "Notable Visitors: Francis Carpenter (1830–1900),"
    Mr. Lincoln's White House blog: www.mrlincolnswhitehouse
    .org/residents-visitors/notable-visitors/notable-visitors-francis
    -carpenter-1830–1900/

McCabe, James D. *The Life and Public Services of Schuyler Colfax, Together
    with His Most Important Speeches*. New York: United States Publishing
    Company, 1868.

Meltzer, Milton, editor. *Lincoln in His Own Words*. Illustrated by Stephen
    Alcorn. New York and San Diego: Harcourt, 1993.

Morris, Jan. *Lincoln: A Foreigner's Quest*. New York: Simon and Schuster, 2000.

Panzer, Mary. *Mathew Brady and the Image of History*. Contribution by
    Jeana K. Foley. Washington, DC: Smithsonian Books/National
    Portrait Gallery, 1997.

Rosenheim, Jeff L. *Photography and the American Civil War*. New York:
    Metropolitan Museum of Art, 2013.

Ruegsegger, Bob. "Confederate's Death Remains a Mystery in Va. Beach,"
    The Virginian-Pilot online (February 3, 2014): www.pilotonline.com
    /news/article_e451c1bc-cba0–5f58-a3a3-f609a8a9bfba.html

Trachtenberg, Alan. *Reading American Photographs: Images as History,
    Mathew Brady to Walker Evans*. New York: Hill and Wang, 1989.

Wead, Doug. *All the President's Children: Triumph and Tragedy in the Lives of
    America's First Families*. New York: Atria, 2003.

Widmer, Ted. *Lincoln on the Verge: Thirteen Days to Washington*. New York:
    Simon and Schuster, 2020.

Wilson, Robert. *Mathew Brady: Portraits of a Nation*. New York:
    Bloomsbury, 2013.

NOTES

1 RIDER IN THE WOODS

p. 5 "not possessed . . . stay at home": Fox, pp. 7–8.

p. 6 "Mr. Lincoln [is] the homeliest": *Ibid.*, p. 4.

p. 6 "He has a face": *Ibid.*, p. 4.

p. 6 "altogether repulsive": *Ibid.*, pp. 4–5.

p. 10 "I leave it": Meltzer, p. 53.

p. 11 "long line": Cornelius, p. 54.

p. 12 "It would be hard work": Fox, p. 4.

2 A FACE TO THE WORLD

p. 19 "very true": quoted by H. Holzer in Kunhardt, p. 25.

p. 24 "photographer's face": Mary Lincoln quoted in Hamilton and Ostendorf, p. 139.

p. 24 "Ah, you want to shorten": quoted by H. Holzer in Kunhardt, p. 26.

p. 24 "Let us have faith": Anderson (editor), p. 196.

3 THE FUTURE IN FOCUS

pp. 29–30 "If you let your whiskers . . . begin it now": Rosenheim, p. 33.

4 CITY UNDER CONSTRUCTION

p. 38 "a factory chimney with the top": Hazelton, p. 63.

p. 40 "huge, grand, gloomy": Goodwin, p. 455.

p. 42 "If people see": Eaton, p. 89.

p. 43 "face and settle": McCabe, p. 154.

5 THE ARTIST IN THE WHITE HOUSE

p. 47 "my best friend": Goodwin, 602.

p. 49 "the Tycoon": Epstein, p. 76. Hay and Nicolay shared this affectionate nickname for the president, having learned it was an honorific associated with the Shoguns, or great warlords, of Japan.

p. 50 "Two o'clock found me . . . I reckon": Carpenter, pp. 42–43.

p. 51 "Well, Mr. Carpenter": *Ibid.*, p. 44.

p. 53 "in the cause of the truth": *Ibid.*, pp. 49–50.

6 FEBRUARY 9: THE PRESIDENT'S MORNING

p. 54 "the shop": www.whitehousehistory.org/lincoln-in-his-shop

p. 55 "Well, wife, there is one thing": Holzer, *Dear Mr. Lincoln*, p. 196.

p. 55 "mutually surpassed each other": Holzer, *Lincoln President-Elect*, p. 364.

p. 57 "I go to bed happy": Carpenter, 172.

p. 57 "Let this man": University of Illinois Library, Illinois History and Lincoln Collections.

p. 58 "wreaked havoc": www.pilotonline.com/news/article_e451c1bc-cba0–5f58-a3a3-f609a8a9bfba.html

p. 58 "I ought to be obliged": Carpenter, pp. 55–56.

p. 58 "I guess we will go": *Ibid.*, p. 56.

p. 61 "startling likenesses of the great": Wilson, p. 54.

7 FEBRUARY 9: THE PRESIDENT'S AFTERNOON

p. 64 "The Lord is": Carpenter, p. 59.

p. 65 "the biggest man . . . as old G": *Ibid.*, pp. 59–60.

p. 67 "You cannot tell": Crain, *New York Times Book Review*, August 2, 2013, p. 11.

p. 72 "third lieutenant": Goodwin, p. 455.

p. 75 "The carriages & coupé": Burlingame, *Nicolay*, p. 126.

8 IMAGES ON THE MARCH

p. 77 "Oh, you need not mind": Carpenter, p. 53.

p. 78 "Absorbed in his papers": *Ibid.*, p. 53.

p. 80 "In my judgement": quoted by Holzer, in Carpenter, p. 10.

CREDITS

Collection; 49 Library of Congress, Manuscript Division, Brady-Handy Collection; 51 courtesy of the author; 53 Library of Congress, Prints & Photographs Division; 56 Library of Congress, Manuscript Division, James Wadsworth Family Papers; 57 Abraham Lincoln Collection, General Collection, Beinecke Rare Book and Manuscript Library; 59 Library of Congress, Prints & Photographs Division, Popular Graphic Arts Collection; 62 Library of Congress, Prints & Photographs Division; 66 National Portrait Gallery, Smithsonian Institution, gift of Larry J. West; 73, 74 Library of Congress, Prints & Photographs Division; 76 Meserve-Kunhardt Collection; 79 Library of Congress, Prints & Photographs Division, Popular Graphic Arts Collection; 82 (left) Library of Congress, Prints & Photographs Division, (right) National Portrait Gallery, Smithsonian Institution; 83 National Portrait Gallery, Smithsonian Institution, Frederick Hill Meserve Collection; 85 Library of Congress, Prints & Photographs Division; 86 courtesy of Abraham Lincoln Presidential Library and Museum; 87 Library of Congress, Prints & Photographs Division, Popular Graphic Arts Collection; 89 Library of Congress, Rare Book and Special Collections Division, Alfred Whital Stern Collection of Lincolniana; 90 Library of Congress, Prints & Photographs Division, Liljenquist Family Collection of Civil War Photographs; 92 Brooklyn Public Library, Brooklyn Newsstand, bklyn.newspapers.com; 93 Library of Congress, Prints & Photographs Division, photograph by Harris & Ewing; 95 National Museum of American History,

Smithsonian Institution, gift of Lincoln Isham, great-grandson of Abraham Lincoln, 1958

Color insert: 1 (top) Library of Congress, Prints & Photographs Division, photograph by Carol M. Highsmith, (bottom left and right) Library of Congress, Prints & Photographs Division, Daguerreotypes Collection; 2 (top) Heritage Auctions, (middle) Smithsonian American Art Museum, Ray Austrian Collection, Gift of Beatrice L. Austrian, Caryl A. Austrian and James A. Austrian, (bottom) National Museum of American History, Smithsonian Institution; 3 (top) Collection of the US House of Representatives, (bottom) Detroit Public Library; 4 (both) Library of Congress, Prints & Photographs Division, Popular Graphic Arts Collection; 5 US Senate Collection; 6 (top) National Portrait Gallery, Smithsonian Institution, Alan and Lois Fern Acquisition Fund, (bottom) Library of Congress, Rare Book and Special Collections Division, Alfred Whital Stern Collection of Lincolniana; 7 (top) Library of Congress, Rare Book and Special Collections Division, Alfred Whital Stern Collection of Lincolniana, (bottom) National Portrait Gallery, Smithsonian Institution; 8 Library of Congress, Prints & Photographs Division, photograph by Carol M. Highsmith

ACKNOWLEDGMENTS

I wish to thank the following individuals and institutions for their help in gathering material for this book and otherwise facilitating my research: Beinecke Rare Book and Manuscript Library, Yale University; Brooklyn Public Library; Gail Buckland; Jim Burgess (Manassas National Battlefield Park); Farar Elliott (US House of Representatives); Meghan Harmon (Abraham Lincoln Presidential Library and Museum); Jim Hays; Anna Hicks (Bonham's); the late Carol M. Highsmith; Carol Johnson; Peter W. Kunhardt, Jr.; Philip B. Kunhardt III; Library of Congress; Lincoln Home National Historic Site (Springfield, Illinois); Mary Todd Lincoln House (Lexington, Kentucky); Metropolitan Museum of Art; New York Public Library; Carla Reczek (Detroit Public Library); Phil Rokus (US Senate); Ann Ruark; Smithsonian National Portrait Gallery; Daniel Weinberg (Abraham Lincoln Book Store); Robert Wilson.

I remember with great fondness and appreciation my late agent, George M. Nicholson, who was instrumental in getting this book off the ground, and I thank his successor at Sterling Lord Literistic, Elizabeth Bewley, for her continued support and encouragement.

A big thank-you and tip of my stovepipe hat to my editor, Wesley Adams, for his wholehearted embrace of this project and for his thoughtful comments and guidance at every stage;

to production editor Lelia Mander, editorial assistant Hannah Miller, copyeditor Linda Minton, proofreaders Kylie Bird and Susan Bishansky, indexer Enid Zafran, and production director John Nora for their uncompromising standards and firm but light touch; to jacket designer Trisha Previte and book designers Maria Williams and Mallory Grigg, and to everyone at Farrar, Straus and Giroux who had a hand in the making of this book.

As always, I thank my family for being my family.

INDEX

Photographs and illustrations are indicated by italic page numbers.